T0129598

An Analysis of

C. Wright Mills's

The Sociological
Imagination

Ismael Puga
with
Robert Easthope

Published by Macat International Ltd
24:13 Coda Centre, 189 Munster Road, London SW6 6AW.

Distributed exclusively by Routledge
2 Park Square, Milton Park, Abingdon, Oxon OX14 4RN
711 Third Avenue, New York, NY 10017, USA

Routledge is an imprint of the Taylor & Francis Group, an informa business

Copyright © 2017 by Macat International Ltd
Macat International has asserted its right under the Copyright, Designs and Patents Act
1988 to be identified as the copyright holder of this work.

The print publication is protected by copyright. Prior to any prohibited reproduction, storage in
a retrieval system, distribution or transmission in any form or by any means, electronic, mechanical, recording or otherwise, permission should be obtained from the publisher or where
applicable a license permitting restricted copying in the United Kingdom should be obtained
from the Copyright Licensing Agency Ltd, Barnard's Inn, 86 Fetter Lane, London EC4A 1EN, UK.

The ePublication is protected by copyright and must not be copied, reproduced, transferred,
distributed, leased, licensed or publicly performed or used in any way except as specifically
permitted in writing by the publishers, as allowed under the terms and conditions under which
it was purchased, or as strictly permitted by applicable copyright law. Any unauthorised distribution or use of this text may be a direct infringement of the authors and the publishers' rights
and those responsible may be liable in law accordingly.

www.macat.com
info@macat.com

Cataloguing in Publication Data
A catalogue record for this book is available from the British Library.
Library of Congress Cataloguing-in-Publication Data is available upon request.
Cover illustration: A. Richard Allen

ISBN 978-1-912303-80-9 (hardback)
ISBN 978-1-912127-09-2 (paperback)
ISBN 978-1-912282-68-5 (e-book)

Notice
The information in this book is designed to orientate readers of the work under analysis,
to elucidate and contextualise its key ideas and themes, and to aid in the development
of critical thinking skills. It is not meant to be used, nor should it be used, as a
substitute for original thinking or in place of original writing or research. References and
notes are provided for informational purposes and their presence does not constitute
endorsement of the information or opinions therein. This book is presented solely for
educational purposes. It is sold on the understanding that the publisher is not engaged
to provide any scholarly advice. The publisher has made every effort to ensure that
this book is accurate and up-to-date, but makes no warranties or representations with
regard to the completeness or reliability of the information it contains. The information
and the opinions provided herein are not guaranteed or warranted to produce particular
results and may not be suitable for students of every ability. The publisher shall not be
liable for any loss, damage or disruption arising from any errors or omissions, or from
the use of this book, including, but not limited to, special, incidental, consequential or
other damages caused, or alleged to have been caused, directly or indirectly, by the
information contained within.

CONTENTS

THE MACAT LIBRARY

The Macat Library is a series of unique academic explorations of seminal works in the humanities and social sciences – books and papers that have had a significant and widely recognised impact on their disciplines. It has been created to serve as much more than just a summary of what lies between the covers of a great book. It illuminates and explores the influences on, ideas of, and impact of that book. Our goal is to offer a learning resource that encourages critical thinking and fosters a better, deeper understanding of important ideas.

Each publication is divided into three Sections: Influences, Ideas, and Impact. Each Section has four Modules. These explore every important facet of the work, and the responses to it.

This Section-Module structure makes a Macat Library book easy to use, but it has another important feature. Because each Macat book is written to the same format, it is possible (and encouraged!) to cross-reference multiple Macat books along the same lines of inquiry or research. This allows the reader to open up interesting interdisciplinary pathways.

To further aid your reading, lists of glossary terms and people mentioned are included at the end of this book (these are indicated by an asterisk [*] throughout) – as well as a list of works cited.

Macat has worked with the University of Cambridge to identify the elements of critical thinking and understand the ways in which six different skills combine to enable effective thinking.
Three allow us to fully understand a problem; three more give us the tools to solve it. Together, these six skills make up the **PACIER** model of critical thinking. They are:

ANALYSIS – understanding how an argument is built
EVALUATION – exploring the strengths and weaknesses of an argument
INTERPRETATION – understanding issues of meaning

CREATIVE THINKING – coming up with new ideas and fresh connections
PROBLEM-SOLVING – producing strong solutions
REASONING – creating strong arguments

To find out more, visit **WWW.MACAT.COM.**

CRITICAL THINKING AND *THE SOCIOLOGICAL IMAGINATION*

Primary critical thinking skill: REASONING
Secondary critical thinking skill: INTERPRETATION

C. Wright Mills's 1959 book *The Sociological Imagination* is widely regarded as one of the most influential works of post-war sociology.

At its heart, the work is a closely reasoned argument about the nature and aims of sociology, one that sets out a manifesto and roadmap for the field. Its wide acceptance and popular reception is a clear demonstration of the rhetorical power of Wright's strong reasoning skills.

In critical thinking, reasoning involves the creation of an argument that is strong, balanced, and, of course, persuasive. In Mills's case, this core argument makes a case for what he terms the "sociological imagination", a particular quality of mind capable of analyzing how individual lives fit into, and interact with, social structures. Only by adopting such an approach, Mills argues, can sociologists see the private troubles of individuals as the social issues they really are.

Allied to this central argument are supporting arguments for the need for sociology to maintain its independence from corporations and governments, and for social scientists to steer away from 'high theory' and focus on the real difficulties of everyday life. Carefully organized, watertight and persuasive, *The Sociological Imagination* exemplifies reasoned argument at its best.

ABOUT THE AUTHOR OF THE ORIGINAL WORK

Born in 1916, **C. Wright Mills** was an American sociologist and professor at Columbia University in New York who had an immense influence on both his discipline and social science more widely.

Mills taught, published books, and was a public intellectual. He was critical of American interference in other countries and of the repressive systems of the Soviet Union and its allies. He was also a leading light in the New Left political movement of the 1960s, and called for a greater role for intellectuals in the social movements that he hoped would transform society and create a new form of socialism. He died tragically young aged just 45, in 1962, of heart problems

ABOUT THE AUTHORS OF THE ANALYSIS

Dr Ismael Puga holds a PhD in sociology from Humboldt University, Berlin. He is currently teaching at the University Diego Portales in Chile.

Robert Easthope holds an MSc in race and postcolonial studies from the London School of Economics.

ABOUT MACAT

GREAT WORKS FOR CRITICAL THINKING

Macat is focused on making the ideas of the world's great thinkers accessible and comprehensible to everybody, everywhere, in ways that promote the development of enhanced critical thinking skills.

It works with leading academics from the world's top universities to produce new analyses that focus on the ideas and the impact of the most influential works ever written across a wide variety of academic disciplines. Each of the works that sit at the heart of its growing library is an enduring example of great thinking. But by setting them in context – and looking at the influences that shaped their authors, as well as the responses they provoked – Macat encourages readers to look at these classics and game-changers with fresh eyes. Readers learn to think, engage and challenge their ideas, rather than simply accepting them.

'Macat offers an amazing first-of-its-kind tool for interdisciplinary learning and research. Its focus on works that transformed their disciplines and its rigorous approach, drawing on the world's leading experts and educational institutions, opens up a world-class education to anyone.'

Andreas Schleicher
Director for Education and Skills, Organisation for Economic
Co-operation and Development

'Macat is taking on some of the major challenges in university education ... They have drawn together a strong team of active academics who are producing teaching materials that are novel in the breadth of their approach.'

Prof Lord Broers,
former Vice-Chancellor of the University of Cambridge

'The Macat vision is exceptionally exciting. It focuses upon new modes of learning which analyse and explain seminal texts which have profoundly influenced world thinking and so social and economic development. It promotes the kind of critical thinking which is essential for any society and economy.
This is the learning of the future.'

Rt Hon Charles Clarke, former UK Secretary of State for Education

'The Macat analyses provide immediate access to the critical conversation surrounding the books that have shaped their respective discipline, which will make them an invaluable resource to all of those, students and teachers, working in the field.'

Professor William Tronzo, University of California at San Diego

WAYS IN TO THE TEXT

KEY POINTS

- Born in 1916, C. Wright Mills was an influential twentieth-century American sociologist*—a scholar of human society and social behavior—who helped shape the left-wing politics of the 1960s.

- Published in 1959, *The Sociological Imagination* proposed a new vision of what sociology should be: a truthful examination of society, uninfluenced by corporate or government funding.

- In 1997 the book was voted the second most influential sociology text ever published.

Who Was C. Wright Mills?

Charles (C.) Wright Mills, the author of *The Sociological Imagination* (1959) had an enormous impact on the history of social science (the branch of scientific inquiry encompassing fields such as anthropology,* economics, history, political science, and psychology).* His powerful writing, particularly in *The Sociological Imagination,* helped inspire and shape left-wing politics in the 1960s.[1] Cultivating a rebellious image—he rode a motorcycle to work and wore leathers while lecturing at Columbia University—he is often seen as the perfect example of a "public intellectual"; scholars have often portrayed Mills as a kind of "rebel *with* a cause"[2] (a reference to the 1955 film *Rebel Without a Cause,** in which James Dean played an aimless middle-class teenager).

Mills was born in Waco, Texas on August 28, 1916. His early academic training at the University of Texas at Austin was in both philosophy and sociology, and his philosophical training later influenced how he approached his chosen discipline of sociology. He was teaching at the University of Maryland by his mid twenties, and became a research associate at Columbia University while still in his twenties. Before *The Sociological Imagination*, he published important books on how society is divided into social classes and who holds power within it: *White Collar: The American Middle Classes* (1951) and *The Power Elite* (1956). These works, widely debated by academics, are still read today. The ideas they contain often seemed to readers to be "a natural extension of his personality: independent, tough, and subversive."[3] They also showed intellectual ambition; Mills liked to "think big."[4] His ideas, along with his readiness to publish pieces aimed at a more general audience in left-wing magazines, helped him gain the respect and loyalty of many young left-wing students and activists.

Outside the US, Mills became a symbol of a politically engaged America during the Cold War*—the period of indirect conflict between the US and the communist* Soviet Union.* His criticism of both American imperialism* (domination of other countries) and Soviet-style authoritarianism* (dictatorship), and his ideas about the role of intellectuals, left a considerable legacy for politics around the globe. In 1968, nearly six years after Mills's death, the Central Intelligence Agency* (CIA) of the United States identified him as one of the most influential figures in global left-wing politics.

His ideas continue to be influential in the twenty-first century: a survey conducted in 2007 of the best-selling sociology textbooks in the US found more references to Mills than to any other author.[5] Many of those references were to *The Sociological Imagination* in particular.

What Does *The Sociological Imagination* Say?

In *The Sociological Imagination* (1959), Mills proposes that sociologists need a specific "quality of mind" called a "sociological imagination." Such an imagination can help create an understanding of the relationship between biography and history—between a person and their specific historical and social context—within specific social structures. Sociology, according to Mills, should turn the "troubles" of individuals into public "issues."

For Mills, many social scientists had forgotten how to do this. He identifies two tendencies in the social science of the day that held back this imagination. One was for researchers to become trapped in their research method: to find themselves able only to work on the questions their empirical* method could handle, rather than the questions that were important to people's lives ("empirical" here refers to methods that draw on measurable, verifiable evidence). Moreover, because employing this method was usually expensive, it brought social scientists into connection with people and powers at the top of society—business executives and government administrators—who could pay for the research. Consequently, researchers tended to study the problems faced by corporations and governments rather than ordinary people. Mills called this tendency "abstracted empiricism."*

Another tendency was for social scientists to become obsessed with solving theoretical problems. This was an issue because ideas were being discussed at such a high level of abstraction (that is, far from their practical relevance) that they were difficult to apply to actual studies and were disconnected from the difficulties of everyday life. Mills called this second tendency "grand theory."* He suggested that the form of grand theory most popular in the US at that time—the "functionalism*" of the influential sociologist Talcott Parsons,* according to which all social customs, structures, and institutions, from family and economy to ritual and religion, should be understood in terms of the practical function they serve—harmonized with the interests of those in power. This was the case, he argued, because of theory's focus on the way existing social relations were maintained.

Mills goes on to argue that social scientists cannot conduct value-free ("neutral") research because values define what a "problem" is. For example: Is income inequality (the difference in income between the rich and poor) a natural part of a modern economy, or a problem to be studied? It depends on your values. So when researchers allow businesses or governments to control which problems they work on, they are, like it or not, supporting the values of those businesses or governments. Social scientists need to be aware of this, and to confront the challenges it throws up; a provider of funds for research, for example, might limit what can be studied.

Mills believes that three values are key to the tradition of social science: truth, reason, and freedom. He argues that the promise of social science is connected to these values, and that social scientists need to decide for themselves how to remain true to them. Only then will they understand their intellectual and political role.

Why Does *The Sociological Imagination* Matter?

When *The Sociological Imagination* was first published in 1959 it was met with scorn from many leading American sociologists. Seymour Lipset* and Neil Smelser,* writing in the *British Journal of Sociology*, were keen to warn British sociologists that Mills's text "has little importance for contemporary American sociology."[6] It was controversial and confrontational.

Much of the book's controversy was due to its fierce criticisms of influential sociologists in America at that time.[7] Sociology has moved on, and today *The Sociological Imagination* is regarded as a key text. This is largely due to Mills's description of what sociologists should be trying to do: to connect the problems of individuals with social issues. He communicates this vision by showing what sociology should *not* be. He warns against working on ideas that cannot be connected to social reality (grand theory), and also against studying data without a clear purpose (abstracted empiricism). While Mills associated these tendencies with the scholars and schools of his day, they are general enough to be found in any time and place.

Moreover, *The Sociological Imagination* addresses wider problems that still exist today. For example, there are ongoing debates about the relationship between social knowledge and power (the question as to whether companies that collect information about our habits as consumers gain too much power, for example) and the political role of social thinkers (should philosophers and scholars help set government policy?). The values of truth, reason, and freedom that lie behind Mills's vision have been questioned by postmodern* theory (an approach to cultural analysis that is skeptical of any universal truths or values), but whether or not this undermines *The Sociological Imagination*'s ability to solve these issues, they remain crucial challenges to consider.

Students and young researchers will also find many pieces of practical advice in Mills's writing. He encourages readers, for example, not to be afraid of making their ideas as clear as possible, suggesting many examples and utilizing work from other disciplines. This is concrete advice for students not just of sociology but of any social science; generations of scholars have found it useful.

In 1997 the International Sociological Association voted *The Sociological Imagination* the second most influential sociology text ever published[8] (after the pioneering German thinker Max Weber's 1922 classic *Economy and Society*). It has been translated into more than 17 languages, has more than 12,000 citations on Google Scholar,[9] and is commonly included in introductory sociology courses.[10]

NOTES

1   Andrew Jamison and Ron Eyerman, *Seeds of the Sixties* (Berkeley: University of California Press, 1995).

2   Daniel Geary, *Radical Ambition: C. Wright Mills, the Left, and American Social Thought* (Berkeley: University of California Press, 2009), 2.

3   Geary, *Radical*, 2.

4   Geary, *Radical*, 13.

5   William Form, "Memories of C. Wright Mills: Social Structure and Biography," *Work and Occupations* 34, no. 2 (2007): 148–73.

6   As quoted in John Eldridge, *C. Wright Mills* (New York: Tavistock Publications, 1983), 110.

7   John D. Brewer, "Imagining *The Sociological Imagination*: The Biographical Context of a Sociological Classic," *British Journal of Sociology* 55, no. 3 (2004): 317–33.

8   International Sociological Association, "Books of the Century," accessed January 13, 2016, http://www.isa-sociology.org/books/vt/bkv_000.htm.

9   Google Scholar, "C. Wright Mills," accessed January 13, 2016, https://scholar.google.co.uk/citations?user=dqBi45AAAAAJ&hl=en&oi=ao.

10 Timothy M. Gill, "'Why Mills, Not Gouldner?' Selective History and Differential Commemoration in Sociology," *The American Sociologist* 44, no. 1 (2013): 100.

SECTION 1
INFLUENCES

MODULE 1
THE AUTHOR AND THE HISTORICAL CONTEXT

KEY POINTS

- *The Sociological Imagination*'s description of sociology* (scholarly inquiry into social structures and behavior) has become widely accepted in the field.

- Mills saw himself as an outsider in relation to American sociology. His intellectual development was deeply marked by World War II* and by the postwar* New Left* in Britain, which opposed both western capitalism* and Soviet* totalitarianism.*

- Events like the Hungarian Revolution of 1956*—an uprising in Hungary, suppressed by the Soviet army— helped convince Mills that intellectuals now had a key role to play in politics.

Why Read This Text?

C. Wright Mills's *The Sociological Imagination* (1959) is a key text in the history of sociology and social science. It challenged social scientists to think about their public role, and it set out what has now become the most widely accepted understanding of what social science should be trying to do: that is, reveal the connection between personal lives and historical developments, and show that connection in the context of social structures (social classes, for example) and institutions (such as the army and the education system). While this vision was at first unpopular with many sociologists in the US, few working today would reject it.

> ❝ Mills's career illuminates, as no other does, the promise and the dilemmas of left wing social thought in mid-twentieth century America. ❞
> Daniel Geary, *Radical Ambition*

The text was also a stinging critique of two trends in the sociology of the 1950s, when Mills was writing: abstracted empiricism* and grand theory.* While the supporters of these trends are no longer active, in part because of the text itself, it is arguable that they represent more general problems in social science's division of intellectual labor. Some scholars are attracted to theory, others to solving specific problems though empirical* (real-world) research. *The Sociological Imagination* reminds us that too much focus on one or the other will lead us away from the core task of social science. For this reason, it remains both an important book and an inspiring call to modern social investigation.

Author's Life

Born in Waco, Texas in 1916, Mills thought of himself as a loner and an outsider in the sophisticated world of academia. His childhood homes had contained few books and little music.[1] When he graduated from Dallas Technical High School, his father insisted he attend a military school, the Texas Agricultural and Mechanical College; but the young Mills, critical of the culture he encountered at the college, transferred to the University of Texas at Austin after one year. There it became clear that he was a gifted scholar; he was even able to publish his first academic article while still a student. His career progressed, and before he was 30, two of the most respected sociologists in the country, Paul Lazarsfeld* and Robert K. Merton,* were "throwing money around" to persuade him to accept a position as associate researcher at the prestigious Columbia University[2] in New York.

Mills's political thinking developed in the context of World War II. While his high blood pressure ruled him out of combat, the war deeply affected his view of the world. As he wrote in 1957, "Following it closely and thinking about it made a radical of me."[3] But rather than the international context, it was the domestic effects of the war that worried him.[4] Mills was a firm critic of the social and economic system of capitalism, and earlier had been a dedicated supporter of the labor movement*—the struggle for workers' rights and a more equal economy. This relates directly to his sense of being an outsider and a misfit: after World War II, intellectuals in the United States had increasingly abandoned radical positions. The growing disappointment with the communism* of the Soviet Union, and the anticommunist policies and repression of leftist organizations in the United States, had severely weakened radical critics.

In this context, Mills's travels to Europe marked an important step in his intellectual growth. In 1956, he received a Fulbright fellowship—a sum of money for international scholarship—to teach at the University of Copenhagen.[5] During the years that followed he traveled across Europe, and found a like-minded circle of scholars with whom he could discuss his critical ideas (his critiques of books, intellectual trends, political developments, and so on). London was of particular significance; he would often visit the London School of Economics (LSE), where he met several intellectuals who would later become identified with what was known as the British New Left. This was "the most significant intellectual connection of his later life."[6]

The New Left called for a new kind of socialism* (a social and economic system in which industry and business are held in common hands) that strongly rejected authoritarian* regimes and the Soviet tradition in general, and emphasized the role of intellectuals in social change. The contrast Mills saw between American and European scholars fueled his already strong criticisms of social science's relationship with power centers in the US. This left several marks on

The Sociological Imagination, in which the critique of bureaucratic*
control, the loss of scientific independence, and the potential for
young intellectuals to transform society are central themes.

Author's Background

Two elements of the political and cultural context stand out as crucial
to *The Sociological Imagination*: the cultural and political impact of the
Cold War;* and the emergence of new kinds of social movements in
the US and elsewhere.

Once Nazi* Germany was defeated in 1945 and the US had
secured its place as a major power, communism was again widely
considered the most serious threat to American society. Political and
cultural life was marked by the Cold War with the Soviet Union.
McCarthyism*—the   hunt   for   communist   sympathizers   in
government agencies and the entertainment industry—had made
anticommunism almost a state doctrine in the 1950s, and socialist (or
suspected socialist) positions were carefully watched. In this context
social criticism became associated with Marxism,* the political
philosophy of the nineteenth-century German economist and
thinker, Karl Marx.* Social criticism was therefore a delicate matter,
and Mills's critical views earned him a reputation as a closet Marxist.

While Mills considered Karl Marx's writings the most complete
analysis of capitalism so far, he also believed that Marxism had been
largely left behind by developments in industrial societies. Most
importantly, he was very critical of Soviet socialism. He saw the Soviet
Union as an authoritarian and bureaucratic society, and distanced
himself from the traditional Marxist beliefs associated with its
supporters.

The Hungarian Revolution* of 1956, violently suppressed by the
Soviet army, and the growing peace and antinuclear movements
strongly influenced Mills and other intellectuals of the time. These
events suggested that students and young intellectuals might come to

play a leading role in political activism (as would indeed happen during the 1960s). Mills was disappointed that the labor movement in the US lacked militancy. He became convinced that it was not the workers, but students and intellectuals who were the most dynamic and important participants in societies on both sides of the Iron Curtain* (the heavily patrolled border dividing the communist Soviet bloc from the capitalist countries of Western Europe). This is reflected in the significance that he gives to a critical analysis of universities and social research in *The Sociological Imagination*.

NOTES

1   C. Wright Mills, *Letters and Autobiographical Writings*, eds. Kathryn Mills and Pamela Mills (Berkeley: University of California Press, 2000), 29.

2   Mills, *Letters*, 84.

3   Mills, *Letters*, 251.

4   Daniel Geary, *Radical Ambition: C. Wright Mills, the Left, and American Social Thought* (Berkeley: University of California Press, 2009), 64.

5   An earlier version of *The Sociological Imagination* was presented there in 1957.

6   Daniel Geary, "Becoming International Again: C. Wright Mills and the Emergence of a Global New Left, 1956–1962," *The Journal of American History* 95, no. 3 (2008): 715.

MODULE 2
ACADEMIC CONTEXT

KEY POINTS

- *The Sociological Imagination* was concerned with the definition of social science itself.

- Mills believed that many of his day's leading sociologists* had abandoned the concerns of classic theorists like the German thinkers Max Weber* and Karl Marx* and become too indebted to outside interests that financed their work.

- Mills was influenced by a number of scholars—especially critics of American capitalism* (the dominant economic and social system in the West); he was also drawn to the independent and critical stance of the New Left* in Britain.

The Work in its Context

C. Wright Mills's *The Sociological Imagination* was written in the tense political context of 1950s America. By the end of the 1950s, the world was clearly divided between the capitalist West, led by the United States, and the communist* East, centered around the Soviet Union,* and by peripheral poor countries that Mills referred to as the "hungry-nation bloc" (commonly termed the "Third World"* or "developing nations.")[1] In the West, capitalist societies, in which industry is conducted for private profit, had finally reached a lasting stability after World War II.* In many European countries this included the development of different forms of welfare state*—systems whereby the government provides services such as healthcare and education free or at low cost to all citizens—and a structured role for labor unions as management partners with the state and business.

> **❝ It is hardly an exaggeration to say that within the sociology profession Mills had gained respect but little support. ❞**
>
> Irving Louis Horowitz, *C. Wright Mills: An American Utopian*

The questions of the time focused mostly on the successes of industrialized capitalism. Had capitalism escaped the contradictions denounced by Karl Marx, according to which struggle between social classes is the principal driver of historical events? Was the world slowly approaching a post-ideological stage in which a single model of society was universally recognized to be the best possible? Were real political divisions, in other words, a thing of the past?[2]

Mills and other left-leaning intellectuals did not think so. They still saw conflicts in the Western, capitalist democracies: for them, capitalism had not really solved political tensions, it had merely hidden them. Challengers to the existing order had been disarmed by force and different forms of manipulation. In *The Power Elite* (1956), for example, Mills stressed the importance of the modern media in this process as a force that shapes political opinion.[3] But at the same time, the Western left was growing critical of the dictatorial and bureaucratic* character of Soviet socialism.* For critical intellectuals such as Mills, it was clear that the Soviet Union's system was not a better alternative. The best option was capitalism—but it needed to change. The key questions were about how to change it, and who could do it.

Overview of the Field

From Mills's point of view, this political context had fed into the main trends in American social science at the time: the functionalism* of the sociologist Talcott Parsons,* and new techniques of "empirical"* sociology.[4]

Parsons's functionalism, taking inspiration from the work of the French social scientist Émile Durkheim,* understood society as a system that depends on the integration of individuals through certain norms of behavior. According to this approach, conflict is only a minor concern for stable societies. For Mills, the theory served more to lend legitimacy to capitalist society than as means to analyze how society functions.

At the around the same time, attention was increasingly being paid to techniques that made use of empirical (roughly, "real-world") data. An important figure in this area was the Austrian American sociologist Paul Lazarsfeld,* who led the Bureau of Applied Social Research at Columbia University when Mills worked there between 1945 and 1946. Many of the studies conducted by this center aimed to show patterns of behavior in society, rather than debating large-scale theoretical models. Mills criticized them for being superficial and small in scope. Scholars who followed this approach avoided engaging in critical analysis, in his view, by isolating their observations from the bigger picture. Moreover, the research questions they chose were likely to be guided by the interests of the organizations funding the Bureau's expensive techniques.

In *The Sociological Imagination*, functionalism and empirical (applied) sociology are held up as precisely what the social sciences should *not* be doing: they serve as a negative contrast to creative and critical approaches to assessing social problems.

Academic Influences

A number of different influences fed into *The Sociological Imagination*. One of these was Thorstein Veblen,* whom Mills considered "the best critic of America that America has produced."[5] Besides a strong critique of capitalism, Mills found in Veblen a direct, combative style that he would himself imitate when writing for the general public.

Such a style went perfectly with Mills's position as an outsider in academia, and with his mocking vision of American scientific culture. This style is very much present in *The Sociological Imagination*.

Another important influence was Edward A. Ross,* an older scholar whom Mills met during his doctoral studies in Wisconsin. Ross was a supporter of eugenics,* a now discredited idea that human beings could be improved through selective breeding. He had been fired from Stanford University in 1900 over his public opposition to the use of Chinese labor in railroad construction in America, and went on to become both a symbol of the struggle for academic freedom and independence and a focus for the criticism of private interests influencing American universities. Noting Ross's story, Mills became concerned with the public role of social scientists and their submission to economic and political powers in American capitalism—one of *The Sociological Imagination*'s most important themes.

Another influence came later, while Mills was writing *The Sociological Imagination* between 1956 and 1958. He was often in Europe at the time, and was greatly affected by the intellectual environment he found there—especially the intellectuals of the British New Left, such as the sociologist Ralph Miliband.* They tended to agree both with Mills's critiques of American capitalism, and his disappointment with the traditional left and the authoritarian form of socialism practiced in the Soviet Union. As well as providing him with space for a discussion of critical theory,* they served as an external comparison for his critique of American social science.

NOTES

1   C. Wright Mills, *Listen, Yankee: The Revolution in Cuba* (New York: McGraw-Hill, 1960), 7.

2   Daniel Bell, *The End of Ideology: On the Exhaustion of Political Ideas in the Fifties* (Cambridge, MA: Harvard University Press, 1960).

3   C. Wright Mills, *The Power Elite* (New York: Oxford University Press, 1956).

4   C. Wright Mills, *The Sociological Imagination* (New York: Oxford University Press, 2000), 82.

5   C. Wright Mills, "The Theory of the Leisure Class," in *The Politics of Truth: Selected Writings of C. Wright Mills*, ed. John H. Summers (New York: Oxford University Press, 2008), 63.

MODULE 3
THE PROBLEM

KEY POINTS

- In *The Sociological Imagination* Mills argues that the idea of value-free (neutral) sociology* is a myth: even the choice of research questions represents the values of the researcher or the funder of the research.

- He sees two main trends in sociology: on the one hand, sociologists being too concerned with theory to analyze real-world problems; and on the other, being imprisoned by their empirical* method (a method drawing on observable, verifiable evidence rather than theory).

- Mills argues that the way to escape this crisis is to employ sociological imagination:* the ability to connect personal troubles with large-scale social issues.

Core Question

Of the many different ideas driving C. Wright Mills's *The Sociological Imagination*, the most significant is probably his questioning of the role of modern social science. While the "sociological imagination" may be an important tool for sociologists, the problem remains as to how exactly its ideas are to be developed and used.

The importance of this question can be considered on two different levels. It is relevant for sociologists because it probes the meaning of their work and their knowledge. But the question is also more universal: the meaning of social science relates, for Mills, to its ability to affect society and, eventually, human history. The critical knowledge provided by social science might grant people the chance to relate their personal troubles to wider public issues: to see the links between their everyday difficulties and social structures and processes.

> **❝** No social study that does not come back to
> the problems of biography, of history and of their
> intersections within a society has completed its
> intellectual journey. **❞**
>
> C. Wright Mills, *The Sociological Imagination*

In this way social science might affect whether "human reason," through the rational analysis of social problems, "will come to play a greater role in human affairs."[1]

Stated in such broad terms, the main questions of *The Sociological Imagination* are as old as social science itself. Mills recognizes this, with much nostalgia, when he describes the classical European tradition: bringing reason into human relations was the basic aim of social studies for the nineteenth-century French social philosopher Auguste Comte,* the nineteenth-century political philosopher Karl Marx,* and the pioneering French sociologist Émile Durkheim,* among many scholars of modern sociology. Although their specific views varied wildly, they all felt reason was closely tied to the ideal of human freedom: in the classical tradition, social thought played an enlightening and liberating role beyond knowledge for its own sake.

Mills claimed that most sociologists had abandoned this classical tradition. In the search for scientific objectivity, mainstream sociology had instead adopted the idea that society can be described in a neutral manner, uncontaminated by the values of researchers or their social context. Mills thought this was impossible, arguing that even the process of identifying research "problems" (or questions) involves values: a "problem" is something that threatens a value you consider important. Mills argued that too many social scientists were concealing this issue from themselves and others—it was time for the political role of social science to be readdressed.

The Participants

For others working in American sociology, the 1950s were years of optimism. Structural functionalism,* an analytical model championed by the Harvard professor Talcott Parsons,* was by far the most influential theoretical model. It proposed that society could be analyzed as a system, with certain functional needs that different subsystems provide for. Meanwhile, new research methods and large empirical research projects—surveys with ever greater scope and complexity—had become possible thanks to technical developments, the growing recognition of sociology as a scientific branch, and sponsorship from state and private donors. This "American" style of empirical research, with its detailed studies of individual milieux* (social contexts), was quickly displacing the broader, more sweeping style of the classical European tradition led by Max Weber,* Marx, Durkheim, and others.

While functionalism aimed at constructing an all-inclusive theory, the new kind of large-scale research focused on solving specific empirical questions. It worked in a predictive way—that is, it predicted outcomes by establishing (statistical) relationships between variables measured at an individual level (age, political position, exposure to radio, and so on), and was strongly marked by methodological individualism* (the idea that social phenomena should be explained by the motivations and actions of individuals). The Bureau of Applied Social Research at Columbia University was the most important research center along these lines. The sociologists Paul Lazarsfeld,* the leading promoter of this type of research, and Robert K. Merton,* a major figure of sociological theory, both worked at the Bureau when Mills was there; the pair published several famous papers together, and Merton's relationship with Lazarsfeld seemed to suggest that the Bureau's empirical research could be linked to overarching theoretical concerns. Mills would later argue in *The Sociological Imagination*, however, that there was no actual paper in which Merton demonstrated how to do this. Mills grew critical of both scholars' work,[2] and left the Bureau on terrible terms with both of them.[3]

The Contemporary Debate

As early as 1943 Mills had already published work critical of this mainstream American sociology. He published an outspoken article criticizing so-called "social pathologists"—specialists who dealt with "individual" problems as "errors" in a normally harmonious system, instead of framing individuals' problems within relations of power and conflict.[4] Much later, in 1953, he continued this line with "Two Styles of Research," an essay criticizing the "molecular" style dominating American social science, in which researchers dealt with "usually small-scale problems" and were often heavily influenced by private and state interests through funding and political pressure. By contrast, Mills described a second form of sociology (which he called "macroscopic* sociology") that tries to comprehend "total social structures" in a comparative and historical manner.[5]

A more defined comparison came in 1954, with the essay, "IBM Plus Researching Plus Humanism = Sociology."[6] Here, Mills distinguished between the main types of sociologists that he would criticize in *The Sociological Imagination*: the "scientists" and the "grand theorists." Both of these are powerful academic groups that, he argues, hold back from analyzing the most urgent social problems. Mills contrasts these two groups with the critical tradition of the Frankfurt school* (a circle of Marxist* thinkers at the Institute of Social Research at the University of Frankfurt in Germany, which engaged in the critical analysis of contemporary society), the "classic" sociologists (including Max Weber and Émile Durkheim), and a selected group of sociologists of his day that he admires. Mills was defining here the so-called classical tradition that would later serve as a blueprint for what he describes in his book as sociologically imaginative work.

NOTES

1   C. Wright Mills, *The Sociological Imagination* (New York: Oxford University Press, 2000), 15.

2   Unlike Lazarsfeld or Parsons, Merton is not mentioned by name in *The Sociological Imagination*. This has been interpreted as a mark of courtesy or loyalty to the theorist on the part of Mills.

3   John D. Brewer, "Imagining The Sociological Imagination: The Biographical Context of a Sociological Classic," *British Journal of Sociology* 55, no. 3 (2004): 321–2.

4   C. Wright Mills, "The Professional Ideology of Social Pathologists," *American Journal of Sociology* 49, no. 2 (1943).

5   C. Wright Mills, "Two Styles of Research in Current Social Studies," *Philosophy of Science* 20, no.4 (1953): 266.

6   C. Wright Mills, "IBM Plus Researching Plus Humanism = Sociology," in *The Politics of Truth: Selected Writings of C. Wright Mills*, ed. John H. Summers (New York: Oxford University Press, 2008), 79–86.

THE AUTHOR'S CONTRIBUTION

KEY POINTS

- Mills argued that sociologists* should cultivate a "sociological imagination"* in order to understand the complex intersections between biography and history in the frame of specific social structures.

- Mills believed social scientists could help shape human society; his book examines the technical, political, and moral problems facing scholars who tackle social issues.

- Although not widely accepted by his contemporaries, Mills's proposal has shaped the way generations of sociologists have understood their subject.

Author's Aims

With *The Sociological Imagination*, C. Wright Mills wanted "to define the meaning of the social sciences for the cultural tasks of our time."[1] He believed that intellectuals play a crucial role in modern societies, and that this role was being threatened by the domination of economic and political powers.[2] His intent was, therefore, to criticize this subordination and outline a social science that could meet the challenges.

Besides this main argument, Mills develops numerous other threads in *The Sociological Imagination*, from the critique of specific authors and techniques to discussing the problem of agency (the capacity to act on decisions and wishes) in human history. While such threads are exciting, and fit well into the book's structure, it is often clear that the work was constructed from different essays, making its general argument harder to follow. Still, Mills succeeds in presenting a

> ❝ I must ask you *not* to mention this [draft] to any of our friends ... I want it [*The Sociological Imagination*] to be just one big dandy surprise: as from a prophet who comes in from the desert. ❞
> C. Wright Mills, *Letter to William Miller*

clear critique of modern social science, and in setting a program for critical and engaged research practice. Such a program is only an outline, and leaves much intellectual work to the student or reader. But a program too specific would damage the principles of craftsmanship and independence that, for Mills, are essential to the sociological imagination: "every working social scientist must be his own methodologist and his own theorist."[3]

Approach
Mills approaches his task mostly by thinking critically about the society and social science of his day. Regarding society in general, he attempts a very general diagnosis of the problems preventing individuals from controlling their own lives. In relation to the sciences, he tries to illuminate how and why they fail to provide answers to these social problems. Rather than giving a detailed description of any discipline, he emphasizes two main trends that can be strongly criticized. These tendencies provide a negative example against which he defines his own position—and in this sense *The Sociological Imagination's* approach can be called polemical (combative); Mills decided to favor strong attacks over absolute accuracy.

Mills also sketches guidelines for how social science might become more relevant in shaping human society. Here, he bases his analysis on his own research experience as well as the example of others; on the critique of the institutional and economical structures of academia (universities and research institutes); and on the technical, political, and moral problems faced by scholars who research social issues. He also provides a detailed account of the planning and writing of his previous study, *The Power Elite*.

Contribution in Context

The role that Mills proposes for social science had only marginal support among the most important sociologists working in the US at that time, including Edward Shills* and Robert K. Merton.* While it may sound reasonable to most sociologists today, it was then generally considered both radical and flawed. Moreover, although he was not alone in criticizing the trends he identified (the thinker Theodor Adorno* was another), Mills was, in general, a lonely figure within American sociology. As such, *The Sociological Imagination* stands alone as a systematic critique of the main threads of American sociology at that time.

Mills's ideas were original, but built on the insights of important thinkers such as Max Weber* and Karl Marx.* Broadly, his sociological imagination allows for an understanding of how the lives of individuals connect with largescale historical processes. He proposes that this understanding does not only serve scientists; the sociological imagination allows for the transformation of individuals' "troubles" into public "issues," empowering them so that they become a "genuine public" instead of a "mass society," and showing them how they can take greater control of their lives.[4] It was this control, Mills believed, that people can increasingly achieve in advanced capitalism.* Sociology's early thinkers, among them Weber and Marx, had spoken with concern about how individuals lose control of their destiny in modern capitalism. But Mills's idea about the special role of "sociological imagination" in combating this loss of control was his own. It can be seen as the result of his early interest in both the connection between ideas and social change, and his personal experiences working as a left-wing sociologist in postwar* America. The gradual development of his position can be seen in the years leading up to 1957, when most of *The Sociological Imagination* was written.

NOTES

1   C. Wright Mills, *The Sociological Imagination* (New York: Oxford University Press, 2000), 18.

2   Mills, *The Sociological Imagination*, 80.

3   Mills, *The Sociological Imagination*, 121.

4   Mills, *The Sociological Imagination*, 187.

SECTION 2
IDEAS

MODULE 5
MAIN IDEAS

KEY POINTS

- In *The Sociological Imagination*, C. Wright Mills addresses four main issues: the task of social science in modern societies; the ways this task has been distorted; the submission of intellectuals to power; and how intellectuals can resist and fulfill the task he lays out for them.

- Mills believed that the sociological imagination* offers an important perspective on the world—and that the key American sociologists had all forgotten how to use this ability to relate the "troubles" of individuals to public "issues."

- Mills presents his vision of social science mainly by comparing it to the two main trends he identifies in the American sociology* of his era: grand theory* (an obsession with constructing theoretical models too abstract to be any use when studying social problems) and abstracted empiricism* (in which data is collected and studied without proper consideration of the theory and purpose behind the project).

Key Themes

C. Wright Mills's *The Sociological Imagination* starts by discussing the promise and the task of social science. According to Mills, social science should relate the problems of individuals to social-structural problems (that is, problems arising from the way society is organized). He calls the ability to do this the sociological imagination, and it is the book's key theme.

> ❝ The sociological imagination enables us to grasp history and biography and the relations between the two within society. That is its task and its promise. ❞
>
> C. Wright Mills, *The Sociological Imagination*

Mills criticizes the social science of his day for failing to demonstrate this imagination. He identifies two types of research that were distorting the task at hand: grand theory and abstracted empiricism. The first abandons real social problems in favor of abstract theoretical models; in the second, "the method" (that is, statistical analysis of survey results and other real-world data) limits the choice of research problems, leading to the study of small-scale questions that remain isolated from their larger context.

Mills next attempts to put these two trends in their social and historical context. He tries to show that they limit intellectuals' autonomy and critical thrust, because they result in researchers coming under the domination of economic and political powers. The main concepts here are "liberal practicality"* and bureaucratic* science. "Liberal practicality" is the mindset of scholars who prefer to study one social milieu* at a time, ignoring the impact of relations with other milieux. This is done in an attempt to record the complexity of social problems by concentrating on a smaller setting, but Mills argues that this approach isolates problems from their structural and historical context. Bureaucratic science, meanwhile, puts scientists under the domination of corporations, state agencies, and the military.

Exploring the Ideas

Five main ideas are key to Mills's analysis of the issues identified above. The first is that the malaise (the sense of unhappiness and not belonging) found in modern societies should set the task for social science. Despite material well-being, in late capitalism* people share a feeling of unease that they are unable to understand: they feel a threat, but they cannot identify it, and so they retreat into inaction. The task of social science is "to make clear the elements of contemporary uneasiness and indifference."[1] The main tool of the social scientist in the completion of this task is the "sociological imagination."

The second main idea is that of the sociological imagination itself. This is a quality of mind that enables us "to grasp history and biography and the relations between the two within society":[2] that is, to understand the relations between large-scale historical processes and the stories and experiences of individuals. Only by looking at individual actions can we fully observe how social structures either change or remain the same. At the same time, however, it is only once we understand how social structures and their changes affect the situations of individuals that we can understand why people feel and act the way they do. It is through the mastery of this complex interaction that social scientists can address their task.

The third big idea is that social problems are defined by the values that individuals and publics cherish; social problems are the situations that threaten these values. While social science needs to be problem-oriented, the difficulty is that values are always involved in the selection and formulation of the problems.[3] The sociological imagination helps by defining problems through the consideration of "troubles" and "issues": the former "occur within the character of the individual and within the range of his immediate relations with others,"[4] while the latter "transcend these local environments" and are related to "the institutions of an historical society as a whole."[5] Individuals are directly aware of their "troubles": the sociological imagination relates these private troubles to public issues, and thereby reveals the problems to be researched.

The fourth central idea is that bureaucratic social science puts intellectuals under external interests and restraints, keeping them from fulfilling their task. Bureaucratic social science serves "whatever ends its bureaucratic clients may have in view," uncritically assuming their "political perspective."[6] Bureaucratic science, he says, produces research with "conservative uses."[7]

The final idea key to Mills's text is "history-making." This refers to the potential for humans to modify their collective destiny. Mills believes it to be stronger in modern society than ever before; at the same time, however, he observes that the "means of history-making are being centralized"—they are being placed in the hands of power elites (the rich and powerful in society).[8] Mills defines democracy in opposition to this power of the elites. Democracy "means some kind of collective self-control over the structural mechanics of history."[9]

The main task of social science can also be stated in relation to history-making and the role of Enlightenment* values (roughly, reason and liberty). From this viewpoint, modern malaise results from "the collapse of the assumed coincidence of reason and freedom"—modernization has not brought freedom to individuals, as we thought it would.[10] The task of social science is, therefore, "to determine the limits of freedom and the limits of the role of reason in history."[11] In other words, Mills invites the scholar to embrace the values of modernity and critically study the limitations of those values. He especially invites them to study what is holding back the realization of reason and freedom. This is the core of *The Sociological Imagination*.

Language and Expression

Mills was speaking, in particular, to young scholars and students of social science. The challenge he set was to produce a critical, imaginative, and engaged form of social science: to reject the technocratic and bureaucratic deforming of social studies, and the useless and isolating jargon (hard-to-understand, specialized language) of scholars. The last chapter of *The Sociological Imagination* is an appendix in which Mills provides concrete, almost personal advice for young researchers: it is a book about sharing the "craftsmanship" of sociology.

Mills was also writing, however, both to youth in general, and to the wider public. To this end, he used a direct and brash style that earned him both the sympathetic label of "public intellectual" and the negative one of "social journalist." Such style is a central aspect of *The Sociological Imagination*; the book includes several examples of "translations" of sociological works into plain and simple language. One result of this was that, while the topics of other works by Mills were probably more important to the general public,[12] few social science books have managed to reach such a wide audience as *The Sociological Imagination*. And of course, the term "sociological imagination" has itself become very much part of academic vocabulary today.

NOTES

1 C. Wright Mills, *The Sociological Imagination* (New York: Oxford University Press, 2000), 13.

2 Mills, *The Sociological Imagination*, 6.

3 Mills, *The Sociological Imagination*, 78.

4 Mills, *The Sociological Imagination*, 8.

5 Mills, *The Sociological Imagination*, 8.

6 Mills, *The Sociological Imagination*, 101.

7 Mills, *The Sociological Imagination*, 100.

8 Mills, *The Sociological Imagination*, 183.

9 Mills, *The Sociological Imagination*, 116.

10 Mills, *The Sociological Imagination*, 169.

11 Mills, *The Sociological Imagination*, 184.

12 C. Wright Mills, *The Power Elite* (New York: Oxford University Press, 1956); C. Wright Mills, *The Causes of World War Three* (New York: M.E. Sharpe, 1958); C. Wright Mills, *Listen, Yankee: The Revolution in Cuba* (New York: McGraw-Hill, 1960).

SECONDARY IDEAS

KEY POINTS

- The secondary ideas in the text include features of sociology* that Mills criticized (grand theory,* abstracted empiricism,* and fetishism of the concept,* according to which the research concept takes precedence over explaining reality), and certain principles he advocated, including the importance of psychological* depth.

- Mills's criticisms of grand theory and abstracted empiricism have had the most influence—arguably helping to cause a sharp decline in their popularity.

- Mills felt deeply that the role of social science is to link private troubles with wider (that is, political) issues.

Other Ideas

From the modern reader's point of view, the core themes of *The Sociological Imagination* are the task that C. Wright Mills proposes for social science, and his description of the problems social science needs to confront. But there are further ideas that are worthy of attention. Of these, his critiques of mainstream sociology in the 1950s are significant; they were controversial at the time, provoking much debate. They draw on original reflections about the role of problems, theory, and methods in social research, and play a key role in the text's central argument. We cannot understand many of Mills's points about the political role of social science, modern sociology's failure, or his proposed solution without understanding his criticisms of abstracted empiricism and grand theory.

It is also important to understand his notions of the "principle of historical specificity," the importance of psychological depth, and his

> ❝ Abstracted empiricism is used bureaucratically, although it has of course clear ideological meanings, which are sometimes used as such. Grand theory, as I have indicated, has no direct bureaucratic utility; its political meaning is ideological, and such use as it may have lies there. Should these two styles of work ... come to enjoy an intellectual 'duopoly,' or even become the predominant styles of work, they would constitute a grievous threat to the intellectual promise of social science and as well to the political promise of the role of reason in human affairs ... ❞
>
> C. Wright Mills, *The Sociological Imagination*

critique of specialization in academia. These core ideas show what kind of research strategies Mills thought the sociological imagination could use in practice—taking concepts and methods from a wide range of sources and disciplines to understand the historical particularity of societies.

Exploring the Ideas

Mills's first critique of mainstream sociology deals with "grand theory." Here, concepts are no longer "used to state more precisely or more adequately any new problem of recognizable significance."[1] Instead, the aim of a grand theory study is simply to build a new concept— something he calls "fetishism of the concept"—thereby turning it into an object of obsession. Often, he argues, the problem stems from ignoring the historical context of the analysis. The grand theorist builds a "trans-historical world," in which concepts lack any "present empirical reference"[2]—in other words, they are not connected to any real part of today's society.

Mills identifies grand theory with the sociologist Talcott Parsons* and his functionalist* "social action theory." Parsons claimed to integrate the views of the classical sociologists Émile Durkheim* and Max Weber* into his scheme. Mills, however, thought that Parsons's interpretation of Weber's work was misleading (a controversial opinion at the time, although now widely accepted). Parsons had, Mills claimed, arbitrarily stripped off Weber's consideration of power and conflict as social forces. Thus, for Mills, Parsons dealt more with "'legitimations' than with institutions of any sort."

In other words: Mills felt that Parsons's aim was to legitimize, or justify, society's existing institutions.[3] In this way, Parsons performed a "magical elimination of conflict," stopping him from "dealing with social change, with history."[4]

The second critique deals with "abstracted empiricism," which Mills identified with the figure of Paul Lazarsfeld.* Mills argued that the researchers involved in this approach were becoming totally driven by "the method" (the statistical analysis of surveys), only daring to investigate questions that came within its scope. The method, however, had been imported from natural science, and was not tailored to face the problems that social science seeks to address; it did not take history into account and tended to avoid problems related to social structures.[5] Moreover, because it was expensive, it required funding from large institutions. As these were generally corporations, the army, or the state, this meant greatly increasing the control of these powerful groups over science.

Mills uses Karl Marx's* "principle of historical specificity" to argue that for a true understanding of what is particular about certain societies, we need to compare them not only with other societies today, but also with societies of the past. He also argues that we need psychological depth: the "problems of our time … cannot be stated adequately without … recognition of the need to develop further a psychology of man that is sociologically grounded and historically relevant."[6] In other words, we need to explore the psychological foundations that push people to act as they do in order to understand how society works.

In his critique of disciplinary specialization, Mills attacks the divisions between different academic branches. He calls for "each social scientist to join social science" in general. Rather than focusing on only one aspect of society (markets, political system, family rules, and so on), scholars should follow the classical tradition, analyzing issues from a broad perspective. This means, when examining any problem, trying to "understand its place within the total social structure, and hence its relations with other institutional domains."[7] Mills tries to show that disciplinary boundaries (between sociology, anthropology,* political sciences, and so on) were "more or less accidentally built," and do not represent any relevant differences now.

Overlooked

Several elements of *The Sociological Imagination* are often overlooked—for instance, some of Mills's first thoughts on the coming of "a postmodern* period" where modern categories suddenly appear "unwieldy, irrelevant, not convincing."[8] The current postmodern period is characterized by the replacement of certainties with doubt—notably with regard to the idea that science and reason are leading us to a better future. Mills talks about the "uneasiness" that this change brings about. He predicts that the new "technological ethos and the kind of engineering imagination associated with science are more likely to be frightening and ambiguous than hopeful and progressive."[9] In this way he spoke early of a crisis in the modern idea of science.

The Sociological Imagination is a discussion of what makes up the sociological discipline—"a universal prescription for the sociological tradition,"[10] according to one scholar. But it also makes a radical political claim that is seldom considered: that the role of social sciences is to translate private troubles into public (that is, political) issues. In other words, the role of social sciences is to unmask the effect of social structures on private life, and thereby to take apart the liberal fantasy that individuals create for their own selves. Social science needs to do this, Mills claims, because people, "in the welter of their daily experience, often become falsely conscious of their social positions"[11]—in other words, they have mistaken ideas about their place in society's hierarchy. Thus the book can be read as a critique of "ideology" in the Marxist* sense: an essay on the rational use of social knowledge to disrupt the legitimization of the status quo. Scholars have yet to write a proper analysis of what *The Sociological Imagination* can tell us about how late capitalism is legitimized by social knowledge.

NOTES

1   C. Wright Mills, *The Sociological Imagination* (New York: Oxford University Press, 2000), 49.

2   Mills, *The Sociological Imagination*, 124.

3   Mills, *The Sociological Imagination*, 35–6.

4   Mills, *The Sociological Imagination*, 42.

5   Mills, *The Sociological Imagination*, 61.

6   Mills, *The Sociological Imagination*, 143.

7   Mills, *The Sociological Imagination*, 138–9.

8   Mills, *The Sociological Imagination*, 166.

9   Mills, *The Sociological Imagination*, 16.

10   John D. Brewer, "Imagining *The Sociological Imagination*: The Biographical Context of a Sociological Classic," *British Journal of Sociology* 55, no. 3 (2004): 332.

11   Mills, *The Sociological Imagination*, 5.

MODULE 7
ACHIEVEMENT

KEY POINTS

- Mills's vision of sociology* is now widely referred to in sociology textbooks and courses.

- The book's rhetorical power is arguably the primary reason for its success.

- Despite being a very "American" work, in the short term Mills's confrontational style made its message hard for prominent American sociologists to listen to.

Assessing the Argument

The distinction C. Wright Mills made in *The Sociological Imagination* between "grand theory"* and "abstracted empiricism"* was controversial. The problem, as noted by Barrington Moore Jr.,* a fellow sociologist who was sympathetic to Mills, was that the contrast was "too stark to give a precise and just picture … [and so] does not convey much of a notion of the richness and diversity in present-day work in sociology."[1]

In an earlier article, Mills had categorized previous sociological work into three streams rather than two.[2] The practitioners of grand theory and abstracted empiricism were left faceless, while those in the third group, called simply "the sociologists," were named, and numerous examples of their research praised. The historian Daniel Geary* argues that *The Sociological Imagination* suffers for not doing the same.[3] Yet it was a conscious decision by Mills to reverse this framing in *The Sociological Imagination*. Here, it is the third group that becomes rather anonymous; and when we compare the two texts, it seems that the structure of *The Sociological Imagination* gives it a greater sense of

> ❝ Mills not only invoked the sociological imagination, he practiced it brilliantly. ❞
>
> Todd Gitlin, afterword to *The Sociological Imagination*

urgency. Grand theory and abstracted empiricism appear intellectually closed in comparison to the hopeful description of a sociology conducted through the sociological imagination. So if Mills wanted to provoke change in mainstream sociology with this work, then it is hard to see how he could have made his arguments better.

Achievement in Context

Mills originally intended to call his book *Autopsy of Social Science*—a far more negative title than *The Sociological Imagination*. He felt that because many of sociology's leading figures had abandoned the "sociological imagination" there was little hope of a revival.[4] Geary suggests that it was the favorable responses Mills received after sending the manuscript out to colleagues that convinced him that the patient (American sociology) had a brighter prognosis than he originally thought.[5] His outlook may have been buoyed by his visit to the London School of Economics in 1957, where he gave three lectures to an appreciative audience of left-leaning intellectuals. In a letter he then sent to the school's director, he observed that "quite frankly, I have often felt the lack of an audience with which I could believe I was truly in communication. Last weekend I came to realize what such an audience looks like."[6] Discovering the British New Left,* who shared his disillusionment with the Soviet* form of socialism,* gave Mills hope for sociology.

Nevertheless, Mills decided to end *The Sociological Imagination* with a warning about the difficulties facing any social scientists who want to make a positive difference: "Our relations with [the powerful] are more likely to be only such relations as they find useful, which is to say that we become technicians accepting their problems and aims, or ideologists promoting their prestige and authority."[7] But Mills's work itself was proof that sociologists could still speak with an independent voice, rising above the systems of power that he had identified.

Limitations

Although Mills's *The Sociological Imagination* holds a message that is relevant far beyond its original setting (the United States of the 1950s and 1960s), the book bears heavy marks of its time and place of origin; these can be categorized into three major aspects.

First, many of the book's critiques and ideas are specific to 1950s American academia—an observation that Mills would probably have accepted and even encouraged, as "every well-considered social study … requires an historical scope."[8] Making sense of some of its concrete analyses, then, requires an exercise in interpretation, especially as we go beyond the post-World War II* period. For example, Mills's description of state involvement in social research may no longer hold (or not outside the US), but the related problems of the bureaucratization* of the sciences (being crippled by rigid or limiting procedures), and loss of autonomy, remain relevant. Similarly, today, after decades of discussion about globalization (the process by which economic, political, and cultural ties are converging across continental boundaries), the book's argument for the relevance of nation states (countries) as the most significant units for "history-making" and therefore for analysis might seem obsolete, or at least simplistic. But the underlying problem—of how to link the analysis of individual people with the analysis of macro-level bodies (that is, large institutions, whole countries, Western society)—remains.

Second, the book entirely ignores social issues that are now central for all but the most conservative sociologists. Mills uses male pronouns, employing "man" as a synonym for "human being" and usually "men" for "humanity." And in its extensive discussion of power relations (roughly, systems of social dominance), the book refers to gender only once, and in passing.[9] The issue of race is not mentioned at all, something particularly puzzling considering the role of the Civil Rights movement in Mills's America: a striking omission that is found across all his books, and for which he has been criticized by even his most sympathetic commentators.[10]

Third, Mills has been rightly described as a "quintessential [model] American"—his radical critique of American society was deeply shaped by distinctively American values and concerns.[11] Concepts such as moral entrepreneurship and individualist independence are used widely in *The Sociological Imagination*, and they are perhaps more useful for understanding the United States than they are for other societies. The book is, in this way, culturally specific.

NOTES

1   Barrington Moore Jr., as cited in Daniel Geary, *Radical Ambition: C. Wright Mills, the Left, and American Social Thought* (Berkeley: University of California Press, 2009), 172–3.

2   C. Wright Mills, "IBM Plus Researching Plus Humanism = Sociology," in *The Politics of Truth: Selected Writings of C. Wright Mills*, ed. John H. Summers (New York: Oxford University Press, 2008), 79–86.

3   Daniel Geary, *Radical Ambition: C. Wright Mills, the Left, and American Social Thought* (Berkeley: University of California Press, 2009), 173.

4   Geary, *Radical*, 175.

5   Geary, *Radical*, 175.

6   Geary, *Radical*, 183.

7   C. Wright Mills, *The Sociological Imagination* (New York: Oxford University Press, 2000), 193.

8   Mills, *The Sociological Imagination*, 145.

9   Mills, *The Sociological Imagination*, 10.

10 Richard Gillam, "'White Collar' from Start to Finish: C. Wright Mills in Transition," *Theory and Society* 10, no. 1 (1981): 11; Todd Gitlin, afterword to *The Sociological Imagination* by C. Wright Mills (New York: Oxford University Press, 2000), 229–42; Daniel Geary, "Becoming International Again: C. Wright Mills and the Emergence of a Global New Left, 1956–1962," *Journal of American History* 95, no. 3 (2008): 734.

11 Irving Louis Horowitz, *C. Wright Mills: An American Utopian* (New York: The Free Press, 1983), 7.

MODULE 8
PLACE IN THE AUTHOR'S WORK

KEY POINTS

- By the time he wrote *The Sociological Imagination*, Mills had already published four major works, including pessimistic studies of the labor movement* (the struggle for workers' rights and a more equal economy), the bureaucratization* of modern life, and the groups that hold power in American society.

- The book was to be Mills's only book focusing entirely on the discipline of sociology.*

- *The Sociological Imagination* may be thought of as the peak of Mills's critique of American society and the practice of sociology; today his reputation rests mainly on this work.

Positioning

By the time C. Wright Mills met his early death at the age of 45 from heart problems, he had produced an impressive body of written work and was internationally celebrated. Even by 1959, when he published *The Sociological Imagination*, he had established himself as a fertile author with a brilliant academic career, and had already published four major works. The first, *The New Men of Power* (1948), was an investigation of labor unions and their leadership. As a radical critic of capitalism,* Mills concluded in this work that labor had been seduced by postwar* welfare policies and was no longer a militant force.[1] This pessimism marked a starting point for Mills's radical sociology: he concluded that Karl Marx's* critique of capitalism was sound, but that his trust in the revolutionary role of the working class, who were expected to lead the fight for a more just society, was misplaced. Social change needed a new and different project.

> ❝ The book's positioning at the core of the mainstream sociological tradition has contributed to the enhancement of Mills's subsequent reputation, but transformed it in the process from a radical critic of industrial society into the prophet of sociology's promise. ❞
>
> John Brewer, *Imagining The Sociological Imagination*

His second book, *White Collar* (1951), was an ambitious analysis of America's "new middle classes."* It featured a stronger emphasis on the alienating and psychologically* destructive effects of modern capitalism, such as the role of bureaucracy in the domination of the masses.[2] The conclusions were as pessimistic as those of *The New Men of Power*, and the tone even grimmer: white-collar workers have been reduced to small "robots" in a gigantic machine, with their ability to be critical or to challenge the status quo completely taken away. The rationalization* of life and work (the imposition of rules and procedures to improve efficiency) has not led to the rule of reason: the enlightened* middle class of the modern period has been replaced by a class of bureaucratic automatons. Where in past centuries, some business leaders may have been educated innovators, today they tend to be uninspired people who stick to the rules.

The third title did not examine a potential challenger to power, but rather the groups that hold that power. *The Power Elite* (1956) analyzed the powerful, and their rule over three "institutional orders": the economic, political, and military. These elites, unlike labor and the middle classes, are described as being organized to promote their own interests: they have a strong shared identity and clear mechanisms for their cultural and material reproduction. In this final diagnosis of social conflict in America, Mills describes the huge political and organizational advantage held by the elites.[3]

After these books, Mills changed his focus and went on to produce hard-hitting works for the wider public dealing with political conflicts: *The Causes of World War Three* (1958),[4] on the Cold War* and the peace movement; and *Listen, Yankee* (1960),[5] a defense of the 1959 Cuban Revolution* and a critique of American imperialism,* which was published after *The Sociological Imagination*.

Mills only published one more book before his early death: *The Marxists* in 1962. Here he analyzed the Marxist* tradition of social and political thought. If *The Sociological Imagination* was a sociological manifesto, *The Marxists* clarifies Mills's complex position regarding the traditional left and Marxism.[6] He often thought of himself as very close to the young Marx,* and in his later years he "became convinced that the real options" for social science "were within Marxism."[7] But Mills's pessimistic vision of the working class and the labor movement, and therefore his view that it was largely intellectuals who should be entrusted with the task of social reform in late capitalism, remained his core political idea.

Integration

The Sociological Imagination is the only one of Mills's books entirely dedicated to his views on sociology. To some extent, it is a stand-alone project; however, it can also be seen as a return to his early interest in the sociology of knowledge. After all, *The Sociological Imagination* is an analysis of the way in which the influence of the powerful affects the production of sociological knowledge, a description of the problem this poses, and a proposed solution.

Sociological knowledge was the subject of his doctoral dissertation under Howard Becker* at the University of Wisconsin as well as his first few published articles. Becker argued that sociological theory and practice needed to remain separate areas of study; so it is not surprising that he was worried about Mills's intention to combine theoretical reflection with empirical* study. It was a source of great conflict between the two. In the end Mills settled on trying to write an analysis of the pragmatist* school of philosophy (a school which, roughly, emphasizes the importance of a hypothesis's practicality), linking the development of pragmatist ideas to social changes. While he was dissatisfied with the result, we can see that it gave a taste of what was to come in *The Sociological Imagination*'s analysis of grand theory* and abstracted empiricism*—in the methodology that both works used, and in Mills's criticism of the notion that empirical and theoretical matters could, or should, be separated.

Putting *The Sociological Imagination* in this context shows that while Mills's other famous books, among them *The Power Elite* and *White Collar*, had a very different focus to *The Sociological Imagination,* the latter was very much part of his intellectual journey.

Significance

The Sociological Imagination marks the peak of Mills's writings on purely sociological issues. Unlike his previous texts, it is not the study of a particular real-world problem; it is, rather, a manifesto in which he outlines his own approach. In many ways *The Sociological Imagination* brings together the scholarly practices of his previous works: a sociology driven by politically meaningful problems to be explored, where theory and method follow the requirements of the questions raised, and not the other way around. It was an opportunity for Mills to develop his vision of politics and history in general, and his express his support for the values of enlightenment.*

Many of these ideas had been present in his early essays. But *The Sociological Imagination* gave them better expression. While this was partly because he had improved his writing style over the years, the position from which he wrote was also important. With a solid catalogue of work to demonstrate his expertise, he was no longer trying to establish himself—he clearly felt able to unleash his cutting wit and rhetoric in *The Sociological Imagination,* despite having become something of an outsider in relation to American professional sociology. According to Google Scholar, the text is now the most commonly cited of all Mills's books and articles; as of 2016 it has over 12,000 citations, far more than Mills's next most-cited book, *The Power Elite,* which has fewer than 7,000.[8]

NOTES

1   C. Wright Mills, *The New Men of Power: America's Labor Leaders* (Urbana, IL: University of Illinois Press, 1948).

2   C. Wright Mills, *White Collar: The American Middle Classes*, 5th ed. (New York: Oxford University Press, 2002).

3   C. Wright Mills, *The Power Elite* (New York: Oxford University Press, 1956).

4   C. Wright Mills, *The Causes of World War Three* (New York: M.E. Sharpe, 1985).

5   C. Wright Mills, *Listen, Yankee: The Revolution in Cuba* (New York: McGraw-Hill, 1960).

6   C. Wright Mills, *The Marxists* (Harmondsworth: Penguin Books, 1962).

7   Irving L. Horowitz, "In Memoriam: *The Sociological Imagination* of C. Wright Mills," *American Journal of Sociology* 68, no. 1 (1962): 106.

8   Google Scholar, "C. Wright Mills," accessed January 13, 2016, https://scholar.google.co.uk/citations?user=dqBi45AAAAAJ&hl=en&oi=ao

SECTION 3
IMPACT

THE FIRST RESPONSES

KEY POINTS

- The most substantial criticisms of the text were that it misrepresented the state of American sociology* and failed to take a morally neutral stance on what makes research good or bad.

- Mills did not respond directly to criticisms of the book.

- Responses to the work in the US were shaped by Mills's hostile criticism of his fellow sociologists.

Criticism

C. Wright Mills's *The Sociological Imagination* was a work of scientific critique—a biting critique, indeed, of some of America's most influential sociologists. So while the reaction from British sociologists was generally positive, the reaction to its publication inside the United States was, unsurprisingly, harsh.

This hostile reaction often had strongly personal overtones; many reviewers in influential journals simply refused to take the book seriously. Compared to a Christian television preacher, Mills was mockingly called "a kind of Billy Graham* of sociology,"[1] a man seeing "himself as shaped in the mold of the great warrior-intellectuals,"[2] and "the caretaker of the dustbin of history."[3] The issues raised in the book were dismissively described as "a matter of surpassing triviality unworthy of the detailed attention of serious men."[4] A few of these reviewers recognized that the problems Mills had identified were crucial, and even saw the value of his intentions, but most of them still denounced his work as a pretentious and self-righteous attack on the discipline.

> ❝ What does this solitary horseman—who is in part prophet, in part a teacher, in part a scholar, and in part a rough-tongued brawler—a sort of Joe McCarthy* of sociology, full of wild accusation and gross inaccuracies, bullying manners, harsh words, and shifting grounds—want of sociology? ❞
>
> Edward Shils, *Imaginary Sociology*

Among the most influential American sociologists who commented on the book was George C. Homans,* a major figure in "social exchange theory"* and later president of the American Sociological Association. Homans claimed to share some of Mills's concerns, but accused him of being unnecessarily aggressive in his arguments. Although, like Mills, Homans was critical of functionalism,* he did not accept his criticisms of research (for focusing on overly narrow social issues), and sociology in general (for claiming it pursued moral neutrality). Homans directs his principal rebuttal to Mills's call for sociology to adopt new norms: despite sharing "these values and so [agreeing] with Mills's judgments," *The Sociological Imagination* goes too far, being "a book that judges different kinds of social science as good or bad according to a set of moral and intellectual values."[5] Homans thought social science should be based on value-free, scientific criteria, rather than the promotion of certain values over others.

Talcott Parsons,* one of Mills's main targets, never responded.[6] Another, the sociologist Paul Lazarsfeld,* however, used his foreword to *What College Students Think* (1960) to settle the score. There, he claimed that Mills attacked empirical* research as a whole, aiming to replace it with a sociological imagination* whose concrete parts were never explained. With enormously ambitious objectives and no concrete methods, Mills wanted, in Lazarsfeld's view, "immediate cures for currently incurable diseases"—an attitude usually promoting "charlatanism not knowledge."[7]

Responses

It is documented that Mills was worried about how his book would be received; he knew that it would provoke heated reprisals. But for the most part he did not respond publicly to these negative reactions. It is known from his letters that he felt many of the criticisms of *The Sociological Imagination* to be simply personal attacks and score-settling rants. To some extent, he was right: Mills's aggressive style earned him many enemies among his colleagues. When asked about why he refused to respond to these criticisms, he would often say that no answer was the only good answer for such unworthy opponents. He never replied to Lazarsfeld, for example, who had accused him of launching an attack on empirical research in general, without offering any concrete alternative. When the sociologist Rose K. Goldsen* sent Mills a copy of Lazarsfeld's critique, he wrote back that "such childish comment" was not "worthy of public answer."[8] Mills did not answer any of the critical reviews in scientific journals (not even that of the sociologist Edward Shils,* which he found particularly offensive),[9] and he often similarly dismissed them in his personal communications.

Together with his radical politics, the personal politics between himself and many other sociologists guaranteed *The Sociological Imagination* a negative response. Without such biographical context, it can be hard for the modern reader to understand why the text was so aggressively attacked.[10]

Conflict and Consensus

Many of the critiques were superficial, dealing more with Mills's character than with the book's arguments. It has been suggested, for example, that the critical reaction to *The Sociological Imagination* was linked to the fact that Mills "fell out with virtually all those who initially helped and admired him, which included most of the establishment sociologists of the day."[11] Mills also had a reputation as a sociologist who was quick to criticize others, and got into conflicts easily. This helps to explain why some of the sociologists who initially dismissed his text would later recognize its importance—Mills rubbed many the wrong way, even if, on reflection, they had to admit the value of his work. The British sociologist John Eldridge* points out that even Shils's angry review ends with him sharing Mills's frustration at sociology's lack of progress and giving a positive judgment on the potential for the sociological imagination to help fix this. He suggests that for Shils, it was a matter of "the wrong man speaking in the wrong tone of voice."[12] It is also telling that the reviews in journals of related disciplines (such as criminology[13] and education)[14] took a very different attitude, generally praising the book enthusiastically.

This, arguably, makes Mills's reluctance to respond even harder to understand. Mills did not accept any of his fellow sociologists' main critiques—which were not many, nor especially difficult to answer— nor did he enter into debate. This may have been because his interests changed so rapidly: by 1960, Mills was already deeply involved in study of the Cuban Revolution* of 1959, in which a dictatorship was overthrown by a socialist* uprising. He never wrote again specifically about sociology, and most of his later works (he would die in 1962) were political rather than sociological.[15] In some ways, *The Sociological Imagination* was Mills's farewell to professional sociology and traditional academic life.

NOTES

1 Ronald Fletcher, "*The Sociological Imagination* by C. Wright Mills," *British Journal of Sociology* 11, no. 2 (1960): 169.

2 Edward Shils, "Professor Mills on the Calling of Sociology," *World Politics* 13, no. 4 (1961): 604.

3   Daniel Bell, as quoted in John D. Brewer, "Imagining *The Sociological Imagination*: The Biographical Context of a Sociological Classic," *British Journal of Sociology* 55, no. 3 (2004): 329.

4   Marvin Bressler, "*The Sociological Imagination* by C. Wright Mills," *Annals of the American Academy of Political and Social Science* 326 (1959): 182.

5   George Homans, "*The Sociological Imagination* by C. Wright Mills," *American Journal of Sociology* 65, no. 5 (1960): 517.

6   Rose K. Goldsen, *What College Students Think* (Princeton, NJ: Van Nostrand, 1960).

7   Paul F. Lazarsfeld, foreword to *What College Students Think* by Rose K. Goldsen (Van Nostrand, 1960).

8   C. Wright Mills to Rose Goldsen, 1960, quoted in Irving Louis Horowitz, *C. Wright Mills: An American Utopian* (New York: The Free Press, 1983), 98.

9   Edward Shils, "Professor Mills on the Calling of Sociology," *World Politics* 13, no. 4 (1961).

10 John D. Brewer, "Imagining *The Sociological Imagination*: The Biographical Context of a Sociological Classic," *British Journal of Sociology* 55, no. 3 (2004): 321–2.

11 Brewer, "Imagining *The Sociological Imagination*."

12 John Eldridge, *C. Wright Mills* (New York: Tavistock Publications, 1983), 110.

13 Hans A. Illing, "*The Sociological Imagination* by C. Wright Mills," *The Journal of Criminal Law, Criminology, and Police Science* 51, no. 1 (1960).

14 Jean Floud, "*The Sociological Imagination* by C. Wright Mills," *British Journal of Educational Studies* 9, no. 1 (1960): 75.

15 Michael Burawoy, "2004 American Sociological Association Presidential Address: For Public Sociology," *British Journal of Sociology* 56, no. 2 (2005): 273.

MODULE 10
THE EVOLVING DEBATE

KEY POINTS

- Mills's criticisms of American sociology* helped to remold the discipline, and his positive proposals have shaped way the subject has been taught to students ever since.

- Although the book did not create a particular school of thought, it is thought to have influenced the "reflexive sociology"* of authors such as Alvin Gouldner* and Pierre Bourdieu* (this is an approach in which researchers pay attention to how their own social position might affect the way they conduct research and understand its results).

- The book also helped inspire the politically radical approaches to sociology of 1960s America.

Uses and Problems

The role that C. Wright Mills proposed for social science in *The Sociological Imagination* was at first dismissed by most of the establishment in the field of sociology—but younger and more critical sociologists felt inspired by it. The work was a major influence on a whole generation of "radical" American sociologists in the 1960s and 1970s, who drew on both Marxism* and other more traditional sociological theories. Although it was not concrete enough to become a manifesto of sociological theory or methodology, the book was an inspiration for many authors and its influence on mainstream sociology would continue to grow with time.[3]

In fact, *The Sociological Imagination* now serves as a reference point defining the qualities of sociology. Mills's goal was "social science as the study of biography [individuals], of history [of the community where the individuals live], and of the problems of their intersection

> ❝ What are the chances of success? Given the political structure within which we must now act, I do not believe it very likely … ❞
>
> C. Wright Mills, *The Sociological Imagination*

within social structure." Today, this approach to the gaining of knowledge is widely seen as something that sociologists should strive to follow.[4] In this respect the text is a great success. There is, however, some irony in making sociological imagination* the mark of sociology as a discipline—Mills was actually endorsing the development of sociological imagination beyond sociology itself, wanting a "unified social science;" but according to his analysis, many of his fellow sociologists lacked the quality of mind needed.[5]

Mills was also an early "sociologist of sociology." His book called for a critical examination of the social relations involved in the development of social science, and for sociologists to critically consider the impact of their own activity and position. *The Sociological Imagination* was arguably "America's best contribution to the ongoing debate about the relationship of scholarship to social commitment,"[6] according to one author. The book thus had a powerful impact on the later development of a "reflexive sociology,"[7] in which the place of sociologists themselves is taken into account, by authors such as Alvin Gouldner and Pierre Bourdieu.[8] Today's idea of a "public sociology," a sociology engaging "publics beyond the university … in dialogue about public issues that have been studied by sociologists,"[9] is also attributed by its backers to Mills's influence.[10]

Schools of Thought

Mills is still a much-admired sociologist, "not only something of a legend within the discipline, but one of the few to achieve celebrity outside of professional circles."[11] His legacy, however, does not include a core of young scholars, trained by him, who could take up where he left off. His "trail is relatively thin, with a vast penumbra [half-shadow] of admirers, a small band of followers, and no successor."[12] He is a hero to many sociologists, a mentor to only a few.

No particular "school" emerged from *The Sociological Imagination* or from Mills's other works. In 1964, two years after his death, his former student Irving Horowitz* edited *The New Sociology*, a book in his honor, collecting essays on his legacy and allegedly applying a "Millsian" approach to various topics.[13] While many of the specific essays were praised,[14] readers had trouble identifying a unified approach connecting them, or a distinctively Millsian "new sociology." What more sympathetic critics found instead was a common admiration for Mills and a shared concern for several key issues.[15] Most of these are found in *The Sociological Imagination*; among them are alienation* (a Marxist* term for the loss of our ability to control our own lives), the new developments of capitalism* (and examples of efforts to create real socialism),* bureaucracy* and the automation of social life, the critique of social sciences in which the values of the researcher and social context play no part in the research, and sociology as a critical science rather than a discipline of social administration.

Other issues, such as imperialism,* war, and social classes, are found elsewhere in Mills's sizeable body of work. In time, then, Mills's legacy became identified not with any sociological theory, but with the attempt to make sociology relevant to the public: a social science engaged with public discussions and controversies.

In Current Scholarship

Beyond helping create this impulse toward critical sociology (a sociology that critiques troubling features of society), *The Sociological Imagination* influenced many important sociologists more directly. It played a central role in what would be called "radical sociology" in late 1960s America.[16] In the spirit of Mills, this is a form of critical sociology closely related to Marxism, yet emphasizing both intellectuals' independence and their central role in capitalism's transformation. These sociologists "try to come to terms with American reality by adopting a mixture of Marxism and traditional liberal sociology."[17]

During the 1960s and 1970s, radical sociologists were very active both in academia and public politics. They formed the Sociology Liberation Movement in 1968, and the next year launched the journal *The Insurgent Sociologist* (known since 1987 as *Critical Sociology*). In addition to Gouldner, they include Rhonda Levine,* Martin Oppenheimer* and Dick Flacks,* and they have certainly changed understandings of what is acceptable in their discipline.

In 1988, Flacks revealed that this group was surprised by their initial successes. The Mills-influenced points of view they developed became mainstream in the 1970s and key members achieved leadership positions in the American sociology establishment. Yet their career successes alone did not have the political significance they had hoped for. Mills, it seems, had overstated the importance of sociology. Moreover, as radical sociologists became integrated into the university system they became more and more caught up in "personal survival, career advancement, [and] institutional niche-making."[18] This all made it more difficult than they had expected to use their academic influence to pursue political ideals.

NOTES

1   Michael Burawoy, "Critical Sociology: A Dialogue between Two Sciences," *Contemporary Sociology* 27, no. 1 (1998): 14; Daniel Geary, *Radical Ambition: C. Wright Mills, the Left, and American Social Thought* (Berkeley: University of California Press, 2009), 38.

2   Alvin Ward Gouldner, *The Coming Crisis of Western Sociology* (New York: Basic Books, 1970).

3   Other books by Mills, such as *White Collar* (1951) and *The Power Elite* (1956), have had more influence on the study of specific sociological problems.

4 C. Wright Mills, *The Sociological Imagination* (New York: Oxford University Press, 2000), 134.

5 Mills, *The Sociological Imagination*, 138.

6 Stanley Aronowitz, *Taking It Big: C. Wright Mills and the Making of Political Intellectuals* (New York: Columbia University Press, 2012), 5.

7 Burawoy, "Critical Sociology," 14; Geary, *Radical Ambition*, 38.

8 Gouldner, *The Coming Crisis of Western Sociology*; Pierre Bourdieu, *In Other Words: Essays Towards a Reflexive Sociology* (Stanford, CA: Stanford University Press, 1990).

9 Michael Burawoy, "The Return of the Repressed: Recovering the Public Face of U.S. Sociology, One Hundred Years On," *Annals of the American Academy of Political and Social Science* 600 (2005): 71.

10 Michael Burawoy, "2004 American Sociological Association Presidential Address: For Public Sociology," *British Journal of Sociology* 56, no. 2 (2005): 266.

11 Charles Derber, "The Mind of the Moralist: Review of *C. Wright Mills: An American Utopian*," *Contemporary Sociology* 13, no. 3 (1984).

12 Steven Rytina, "Youthful Vision, Youthful Promise, Through Midlife Bifocals: C. Wright Mills' 'White Collar' Turns 50," *Sociological Forum* 16, no. 3 (2001): 563.

13 For the relationship between Irving Louis Horowitz (1929–2012) and Mills, see John H. Summers, "The Epigone's Embrace: Irving Louis Horowitz on C. Wright Mills," *Minnesota Review* 68 (2007); and Irving L. Horowitz, ed., *The New Sociology: Essays in Social Science and Social Theory in Honor of C. Wright Mills* (New York: Oxford University Press, 1964).

14 Robert Bierstedt, "Review of *The New Sociology*," *American Sociological Review* 30, no. 2 (1965); Joseph S. Roucek, "Review of *The New Sociology*," *The Western Political Quarterly* 17, no. 3 (1964).

15 Arthur K. Davis, "Review of *The New Sociology*," *Annals of the American Academy of Political and Social Science* 359 (1965); Floyd N. House, "Review of *The New Sociology*," *Social Forces* 43, no. 2 (1964).

16 Tamar Pitch, "The Roots of Radical Sociology," *Critical Sociology* 4, no. 4 (1974): 45.

17 Pitch, "Roots of Radical Sociology," 54.

18 Flacks, "Sociology Liberation," 17.

IMPACT AND INFLUENCE TODAY

KEY POINTS

- Today, *The Sociological Imagination* is widely considered to define the features specific to sociological* research.

- The book challenges sociologists who subscribe to postmodern* thought (an approach that treats ideas of objectivity with suspicion).

- Although modern critics have criticized Mills for not giving the voice of individuals a larger role in his vision of sociology, for Mills, sociologists must confront the "moral dilemma" of listening to individuals while seeing the larger social mechanisms behind their voices.

Position

In 1960 C. Wright Mills was "the sociologist of the New Left."*[1] A scholar-activist, fiercely critical of mainstream sociology, his name was linked with socialism* and the critique of oppression, capitalism,* and imperialism.* But today his name rings different bells. Mills became a hero of sociology as a profession, the man who outlined the discipline's preferred role for the late twentieth century and beyond—a reputation he owes to *The Sociological Imagination* alone. Of his many books, it is the most referenced, discussed, and generally influential today, and has been since at least the 1980s. His discussion of sociological thought became his most important legacy.

The popular view of *The Sociological Imagination* itself has evolved since the early 1960s. At that time, the book represented an aggressive critique of the academic mainstream. Today it is mostly considered a "contemporary classic" of American sociology: a work defining the

> **❝** Amongst mainstream sociology, the book is perceived as a universal prescription for the sociological tradition as formally taught, transcending its modernist narrative and language. The essential timelessness of this tradition, the continuity in the way it is constructed from the classics to today, has allowed *The Sociological Imagination* to remain central to the way it is defined. **❞**
>
> John Brewer, *Imagining* The Sociological Imagination: *The Biographical Context of a Sociological Classic*

specific character and mindset of the discipline, beyond methods and theories. For modern scholars, *The Sociological Imagination* defines the current sociological mainstream: it stands "among the most recognized books in the history of American Sociology"[2] and crucially "distinguishes [the] field from the other social sciences."[3] The book is regularly mentioned in introductory textbooks and included on reading lists for sociology courses.[4]

Interaction

The Sociological Imagination is often taught as an optimistic call for more creative social sciences. Its critique of some of the most important sociological traditions is often glossed over or downplayed, as are its radical arguments against sociologists' submission to bureaucratic* interests.

Some of this is understandable: arguably, corporations and state agencies now have less interest in sociological knowledge as a means of social control, turning more frequently to different kinds of experts.[5] The threats to the relevance of social science are also different now. Yet, despite its age, the text can still challenge some contemporary currents in sociology. The sociologist and writer Todd Gitlin,* for example, claims in his afterword to a recent edition that Mills "would be amused at the way in which many postmodernists, Marxists,* and feminists have joined the former grandees [notable figures] of theory on their 'useless heights,' claiming high seriousness as well as usefulness for their pirouettes and performances, their monastic and masturbatory exercises."[6] In other words, *The Sociological Imagination's* critiques of "grand theory"* may now apply to a type of "critical theory"* (an approach to the analysis of culture and society that frequently discusses things such as the cultural consequences of capitalism) that seems more concerned with the sophistication of its concepts than with actually explaining social problems.

In more specific terms, *The Sociological Imagination* has been reframed as a possible critique of postmodern social theory—particularly that of the French philosopher and social theorist Michel Foucault.* Mills emphasizes a theory of elites and bureaucratic power in which the masses, even if currently dominated, must attempt to regain control of their lives. They should do this by using reason and knowledge to understand the social structures oppressing them. Foucault instead poses a broad notion of power ("Power is everywhere; not because it embraces everything but because it comes from everywhere,")[7] and a rather pessimistic view of the role of knowledge ("the power relations give rise to a possible corpus of knowledge, and knowledge extends and reinforces the effects of this power.")[8] Present-day scholars of Mills have denounced the paralyzing effects of Foucault's approach to power.[9] Others find Mills's typically twentieth-century vision of knowledge overly optimistic.[10]

The Continuing Debate

The enlightened* values of rationality and the desire for truth that Mills defends have lost favor within social science. There exists a small "Millsian" group of scholars who want to reinterpret and rescue some of Mills's ideas for a radical sociology; but they are not a major trend in critical sociology today and many of them have given up defending

Mills's modernist* claims ("modernism" was a broad-reaching cultural movement of the late nineteenth and early twentieth centuries; Mills's work draws on modernist assumptions with regard to certainty and objectivity).

In 1990, the sociologist Norman K. Denzin* made a postmodern critique of *The Sociological Imagination* and its modernist tone, judging it "unsuited to the problems now confronting sociology."[11] His main point is that Mills called for a sociology that understands the problems of individuals—which stands for the "little people"—but did not allow these little people to speak for themselves.[12] The challenge is real. Even if Mills considered the voices of those he studied (as he effectively did in his research), putting together their troubles and the related social issues was reserved for him as an intellectual. This was lonely work, and necessarily so, because ordinary, or "little," people are often unable to see what their real troubles are.

Mills was aware of the dangers of this position, and he clearly warned the reader to avoid the authoritarian* (dictatorial) impulses it could promote—he was certainly not as naïve as Denzin makes him look. For Mills, that was exactly "the major moral dilemma" for any self-aware social scientist: in "the difference between what men are interested in and what is to men's interest."[13] By pursuing the former, sociologists accept the same manipulations they want to uncover (the ideas and concerns promoted by big business and government—often to divert people's attention from the fact that they were dominated by those groups). It is a difficult tightrope to walk. By simply accepting these manipulated ideas, sociologists give up their critical task. On the other hand, ignoring the former for the sake of the latter, they risk instead "violating democratic values" and becoming "manipulators or coercers."[14]

Mills's solution to this dilemma is to focus on the relationship between private troubles and public issues. The key, again, is in the sociological imagination*—the quality of mind that enables us to make such links. The question remains as to whether this is a convincing enough solution.

NOTES

1   Jean Floud, "*The Sociological Imagination* by C. Wright Mills," *British Journal of Educational Studies* 9, no. 1 (1960): 75.

2   Steven P. Dandaneau, "Sisyphus Had It Easy: Reflections of Two Decades of Teaching *The Sociological Imagination*," *Teaching Sociology* 37, no. 1 (2009): 8.

3   Norman K. Denzin, "*The Sociological Imagination* Revisited," *The Sociological Quarterly* 31, no. 1 (1990): 1.

4   Timothy M. Gill, "'Why Mills, Not Gouldner?' Selective History and Differential Commemoration in Sociology," *The American Sociologist* 44, no. 1 (2013): 100.

5   Michael Burawoy, "Open Letter to C. Wright Mills," *Antipode* 40, no. 3 (2008): 372.

6   Todd Gitlin, afterword to *The Sociological Imagination* by C. Wright Mills (New York: Oxford University Press, 2000), 229–42.

7   Michel Foucault, *The History of Sexuality* (New York: Vintage, 1976), 93.

8   Michel Foucault, *Discipline and Punish: The Birth of the Prison* (New York: Vintage, 1975), 29.

9   Gitlin, afterword to *The Sociological Imagination*, 236.

10 Burawoy, "Open Letter to C. Wright Mills," 369.

11 Denzin, "*The Sociological Imagination* Revisited," 2.

12 Denzin, "*The Sociological Imagination* Revisited," 4.

13 C. Wright Mills, *The Sociological Imagination* (New York: Oxford University Press, 2000), 193.

14 Mills, *The Sociological Imagination*, 194.

WHERE NEXT?

KEY POINTS

- It is likely that Mills's text will continue to define the particular features of the sociologists' discipline.
- The book's impact will be felt in the work of generations of sociologists who have read his work as undergraduate and graduate students.
- The work has played a key role in both the history of sociology* and left-wing politics.

Potential

Will C. Wright Mills's *The Sociological Imagination* continue to influence social scientists and intellectuals? To what extent are its main ideas still relevant? Many authors have given negative answers to these questions.

Mills's argument is based on a concept of science that, in the view of many, is too naïve to guide social research today. He took the side of the "little people," proposing that we could objectively find the intersections between their ordinary problems and the social structures they could not see. Today, this idea is questioned.[1] Mills took the values of reason and freedom as a basis for his proposal, but do those values have clearly defined, universally agreed meanings? He certainly lacks explanations of what exactly reason and freedom mean to him.[2] Furthermore, social science has changed significantly since Mills wrote his book—to some extent, because of critiques such as his own—and the criticisms of sociology that we find in *The Sociological Imagination* might not hold as clearly now.

The extent to which *The Sociological Imagination* remains relevant in the face of these arguments is open to discussion. However, the

> **❝ At the turn of the millennium, most of** *The*
> *Sociological Imagination* **remains as valid, and necessary,**
> **as ever. ❞**
> Todd Gitlin, afterword to *The Sociological Imagination*

book contains important arguments on issues that remain pressing matters for social science today.

A very relevant issue is whether Mills's specific critique of 1950s-era "grand theory"* and "abstracted empiricism"* represents a more general critical argument that we could still raise today against mainstream sociology. For those who believe that it does, his argument remains valid beyond the particular controversies in which he engaged. Grand theory and abstracted empiricism may be historical forms of sociology that no longer exist as Mills analyzed them, but the argument points to general problems in professional social sciences. There is a conflict between forms of specialization and the division of intellectual labor on the one hand, and the task of solving pressing social problems on the other. This conflict seems to push research efforts in opposite directions. And as long as the conflict remains, *The Sociological Imagination* will retain a measure of relevance.

Future Directions

There are countless sociologists who recognize *The Sociological Imagination* as a major influence in defining the task of their discipline. This definition—"to grasp history and biography and the relations between the two within society"[3]—became so influential that it is now widely used as a basic explanation of the discipline in textbooks, rather than being associated with any particular "school" of thought.

Still, an important yet varied group of American critical sociologists can be identified as Mills's followers. Like Mills, their critical sociology is inspired by the European classical tradition (particularly Karl Marx* and Max Weber,* but also the Frankfurt school* and Pierre Bourdieu*), as well as by an American tradition in which the author of *The Sociological Imagination* now plays a central role.

Mills's ideas on the public role of intellectuals have gained renewed attention lately, as critical sociology turns once again to the problem of the relevance of social studies to public life. Sociologists like Michael Burawoy,* for example, have developed the concept of a "public sociology," which helps bring about public discussion of policies and conflicts. Craig Calhoun* has called for a social science oriented to dealing with concrete problems in society, and in *Toward a More Public Social Science* (2004) he calls for a publicly engaged sociology close to the spirit and argument of Mills's *The Sociological Imagination*.

Summary

Mills's *The Sociological Imagination* is a crucial text for sociology and, more generally, for social science and present-day social thought.

First, it has played a key role in sociology's history. *The Sociological Imagination* had a powerful impact on American social science, challenging what was then a well-established school of thought. This school of thought had two major features: it pushed to professionalize the discipline—distancing sociologists from the classic roles of social critic and public intellectual; and it had a theoretical outlook that paid little attention to conflicts and historical change. Mills's book was neither the first nor the only text to denounce the political consequences of this kind of sociology, but it was possibly the most influential one; it urged social scientists to be agents of change and debate in political and social discussions beyond academia. The professionalization of social science is, arguably, permanent. But the total retreat of social theory and research from public debate seems, today, almost as unlikely.

The Sociological Imagination is also crucial because of its impact on our current definition of sociology as a discipline. Mills, formerly an outsider, wrote a book that was voted the second most influential sociology text by members of the International Sociological Association in 1997. Its main proposal—the importance of a focus on the intersection between personal lives and historical processes in the context of social structures—became today's basic understanding of what social science should work to reveal.

Finally, the book is significant because of its political impact. Mills and *The Sociological Imagination* had a tremendous influence on the new leftist social movements during the second half of the twentieth century. A new kind of critical theory,* focusing as much on the effects of capitalism in rich countries as on economic and political exploitation and control across the globe, found in this book an inspiring manifesto. The book also made C. Wright Mills a popular symbol for the engaged intellectual. Understanding Mills and his book is, in part, an exercise in modern political history.

NOTES

1   Norman K. Denzin, "*The Sociological Imagination* Revisited," *The Sociological Quarterly* 31, no. 1 (1990).

2   Mervyn Frost, "The Role of Normative Theory in IR," *Millennium – Journal of International Studies* 23, no. 1 (1994): 109–10.

3   C. Wright Mills, *The Sociological Imagination* (New York: Oxford University Press, 2000), 6.

GLOSSARY

GLOSSARY OF TERMS

Abstracted empiricism: Mills's term for a style of social research in which data is collected and studied without proper consideration of the theory and purpose behind the project.

Alienation: as conceived by the German political philosopher Karl Marx, the loss of people's ability to control their own lives in a hierarchical society, particularly in capitalism: workers are separated from their work and therefore defrauded of the results of their own human action.

American Sociological Association: the United States's professional body for sociologists, founded to advance the discipline as a positive social influence.

Anthropology: scientific inquiry into humankind, commonly conducted through research into human society, culture, belief, and so on.

Authoritarianism: a political practice, ideal, or system in which individual freedom is held to be less important than obedience to authority. Authoritarian political systems place power in the hands a small elite or single person whom the citizens cannot displace through any democratic process.

Bourgeoisie: the middle class. In social and political theory, the term is used by Marxists to describe the social class that monopolizes the benefits of modernization to the detriment of the proletariat.

Bureaucracy: a complicated administration system or a body of unelected government officials.

Capitalism: a term used of a broad range of modern societies that are based on the idea of individual property and capital. In these societies, business, services, even important state institutions, are held in private hands and exercised for private profit.

Central Intelligence Agency (CIA): a US federal agency, founded in 1947, responsible for the collection, analysis, and distribution of information about national security and foreign intelligence. The CIA has engaged in covert interventions in foreign countries.

Cold War: a term used to describe the political conflict, conducted through indirect means, after World War II between the United States (and its allies) and the Soviet Union (and its allies). It is often said to have lasted from 1947 to 1991.

Communism: a socioeconomic theory or system whereby the community, and not private individuals, owns property and the means of industrial production.

Communist bloc (or Eastern bloc): a term used to denote the USSR and its political allies.

Critical theory: in sociology, critical theory refers to the Frankfurt school's neo-Marxist social theory and philosophy. Critical theorists look to use an interdisciplinary approach to produce research that works towards human emancipation.

Cuban Revolution: a revolutionary movement that overthrew dictator Fulgencio Batista in 1959 by means of armed struggle. Fidel Castro and the other leaders of the revolution later formed a socialist republic in Cuba, which Mills saw as a possible third alternative to the choice between American capitalism and Soviet socialism during the Cold War.

Empirical: concerned with knowledge gained from observation rather than theory.

Enlightenment: a Western intellectual movement, prominent in the eighteenth century, characterized by its opposition to Church authority and its pursuit and celebration of progress, liberty, fraternity, and tolerance.

Eugenics: the idea that the genetic makeup of the human species, or of particular "races" could, and should, be improved through methods such as selective breeding, and sterilization of "inferior" individuals.

Fetishism: generally means attaching supernatural properties to objects. In Mills's "fetishism of the concept," the "concept" no longer exists to explain reality, but is there for its own sake—it has become separated from reality. Marx used the term "commodity fetishism" to describe the process in capitalism through which the properties of human activity are mistaken for properties of commodities and their exchange.

Frankfurt school: a group of Marxist and post-Marxist critical thinkers who worked, originally, at the Institute of Social Research at the University of Frankfurt in Germany. They distanced themselves from orthodox Marxism, greatly influencing contemporary critical theory. Theodor Adorno, Herbert Marcuse, and later Jürgen Habermas are some of the most famous thinkers associated with this school.

Functionalism: a sociological approach, closely associated with Talcott Parsons, that analyses social institutions (such as the family, religion, and the economy) in terms of their role in society. Because each social institution is treated as if it were one cog in the machine of society, functionalist accounts are generally more interested in explaining social order than social conflict.

Grand theory: Mills's term for social research that becomes obsessed with constructing theoretical models too abstract to be any use when studying social problems.

Hungarian Revolution (1956): a failed popular uprising against the Soviet-supported government of Hungary. Its brutal repression by the Hungarian Secret Police and the Soviet army had a strong negative impact on the international image of the Soviet regime, arguably marking the start of the crisis and eventual downfall of the USSR in 1991.

Ideology: a set of political beliefs, ideals and doctrines.

Imperialism: the endorsement and/or practice of extending a state's economic and/or political control beyond current limits.

Iron Curtain: the heavily patrolled border dividing the communist Soviet bloc from the capitalist countries of Western Europe during the Cold War.

Labor movement: the name for a coalition of workers' organizations and political figures and parties struggling for the rights of laborers and for a more equal economy.

Legitimation: a concept popularized in sociology by Max Weber. It refers to the stabilization of power relations by the collective belief in the "legitimacy" of these relations.

Liberal practicality: the mindset of scholars who choose to study one social milieu at a time, instead of looking at the wider context.

Macroscopic view: a view that focuses on large units.

Marxism: a world view and form of socioeconomic inquiry rooted in the economic theory of the nineteenth-century economist and political theorist Karl Marx, and the industrialist Friedrich Engels. Marx saw history as being driven by economic forces and characterized by a struggle between classes.

McCarthyism: a term named after former US senator Joseph McCarthy's campaign to root out supposed communist sympathizers in government and Hollywood film jobs in the 1950s. It means making unsubstantiated accusations of treason or political subversion.

Methodological individualism: the idea that social phenomena should be explained by the motivations and actions of individuals.

Milieu/milieux: milieux is the plural form of "milieu" ("environment" in French). This term is often used in English and other languages to refer specifically to a social environment. Mills uses it to define the immediate environments in which individuals are located and with which they interact.

Nazism: a totalitarian political movement led by Adolf Hitler, the head of the Nazi Party, who ruled Germany between 1933 and 1945. Nazism was characterized by fervent nationalism, dictatorial rule, state control of the economy, military expansion in Europe, and brutal anti-Semitism, which resulted in the systematic extermination of six million Jews during World War II.

New Left: an intellectual and political movement of the 1960s that took its name from an open letter by Mills: *Letter to the New Left* (1960). The New Left attempted to update socialist ideas, and relied more on students and intellectuals than on the labor movement.

New middle classes: in Mills's time, "new middle classes" referred to the salaried classes of bureaucrats and clerks.

Positivism: a philosophy that regards only scientifically verifiable facts and laws as authoritative.

Postmodernism: in philosophy, postmodernism refers to a school of thought best defined by its skepticism about the values and assumptions of (Western) modernity—particularly the power of reason.

Postwar: this refers to the period that followed World War II.

Practicality: the feasibility and real-world character of a task or object. Mills used the concept to emphasize forms of science that work within the status quo in a pragmatic way, rather than questioning it.

Pragmatist philosophy: an approach that considers the exercise of philosophy to have a practical function, emphasizing philosophy as a tool for the solution of material problems.

Psychology: the branch of science dealing with the operations of the human mind and behavior.

Rationalization: in the sociological tradition of Max Weber, this is the rational optimization of administrative, political, and economic processes: it is a rationalization of means, not necessarily of ends.

Rebel Without a Cause: the name of a Hollywood film from 1955 about the aimless lives of middle-class teenagers in postwar America. It starred James Dean.

Reflexive sociology: sociology in which researchers pay attention to the way their own social position might affect how they conduct research and understand its results.

Social exchange theory: a theory that understands social interactions as interchanges of different values, from economic resources to prestige or recognition, and explains social groups and structures by examining the logic of such interactions.

Socialism: a political and economic theory of social organization that calls for the means of production (tools and resources), distribution, and exchange to be owned or regulated by the community as a whole.

Sociological imagination: an ability to relate the small-scale troubles of individuals with large-scale social issues and historical developments.

Sociology: scholarly inquiry into the history, nature, and functioning of human society, and of social behavior.

Soviet Union: the Union of Soviet Socialist Republics (USSR) was founded in 1922 and dissolved in 1991. It was a one-party state whose principles and industrial infrastructure were communist.

Third World: countries not aligned with the US or the Soviet Union during the Cold War were called Third World countries. As many of these countries were very poor, the term began to be used to describe all developing countries.

Totalitarian: a system of government in which the government intercedes in the lives of its citizens and in which dissent is aggressively prohibited.

Welfare states: capitalistic regimes in which a market economy is supplemented with a state-funded system of social protection and service provision, thereby attempting to secure a certain level of welfare for citizens.

World War II: a global conflict that took place between 1939 and 1945 and involved many nations around the world. America entered the conflict in 1941; the war ended with the defeat of Germany and her allies and the dropping of two atomic bombs on Japan.

"Young Marx": in the context of Marxist literature, the early works of Karl Marx. These had a stronger emphasis on the problems of alienation within society, ideology, and consciousness than his later works (which focused instead on socioeconomic structures of human existence).

PEOPLE MENTIONED IN THE TEXT

Theodor W. Adorno (1903–69) was a German critical sociologist and philosopher, and a major figure of the famous Frankfurt School. His works include some of the most influential treatises on critical theory in the past century, such as the *Dialectic of Enlightenment* (1947) and *Negative Dialectics* (1966).

Ulrich Beck (1944–2015) was a prominent German sociologist, best known for the concept of "risk society." His works include *Risk Society: Towards a New Modernity* (1992) and *Reflexive Modernization* (1994).

Howard P. Becker (1899–1960) was C. Wright Mills's thesis supervisor at the University of Wisconsin–Madison. Works include *Man in Reciprocity: Introductory Lectures on Culture, Society and Personality* (1956).

Pierre Bourdieu (1930–2002) was a French sociologist and ethnographer, probably one of the most influential social thinkers of the late twentieth century. He is particularly famous for his theory of social "fields" and "capitals." His most important works include *Distinction* (1979), *Practical Reason* (1994) and *Pascalian Meditations* (2000).

Michael Burawoy (b. 1947) is a well-known British sociologist, president of the International Sociological Association (ISA) between 2010 and 2014, and a declared follower of Mills's legacy. His best-known work is *Manufacturing Consent: Changes in the Labor Process under Monopoly Capitalism* (1979).

Craig Calhoun (b. 1952) is a prominent American critical sociologist, the director of the London School of Economics and Political Science, and the president of the Social Science Research Council. His most influential works include *Nationalism* (1997) and *Critical Social Theory* (1995).

Auguste Comte (1798–1857) was a French positivist philosopher, and a founder of sociology as a discipline. He promoted the role of science as a rational means of improving social organization.

Norman K. Denzin (b. 1941) is a professor at the University of Illinois, and a major figure in qualitative sociology. He coedited the widely used *The Sage Handbook of Qualitative Research* (2005), and is known for his studies of alcoholism.

Émile Durkheim (1858–1917) was a French social scientist who contributed significantly to the establishment of sociology as a scientific discipline. His work strongly influenced functionalism, and his most famous works include *The Division of Social Labor* (1893), *The Rules of Sociological Method* (1895), *Suicide* (1897), and *The Elementary Forms of Religious Life* (1912).

John Eldridge is a British sociologist. He has written books on C. Wright Mills and Max Weber, and is well known for his work analyzing television news. Works include *Getting the Message: News, Truth and Power* (1993).

Richard "Dick" Flacks (b. 1938) recently retired as professor emeritus of sociology at the University of California in Santa Barbara, where he had taught since 1969. A lifetime social activist, he wrote *Making History: The American Left and the American Mind* (1988).

Michel Foucault (1926–84) was a French sociologist and philosopher, and one of the main figures of French postmodernism. His most famous works include *Discipline and Punish* (1975) and *The History of Sexuality* (1976).

Daniel Geary is Mark Pigott Associate Professor of US History at Trinity College, Dublin. In addition to his biography of C. Wright Mills, he has recently published *Beyond Civil Rights: The Moynihan Report and Its Legacy* (2015).

Todd Gitlin (b. 1943) is an American sociologist and public intellectual. As well as his academic studies of mass communications, he has also written numerous books and hundreds of news articles aimed at a wider audience. These include *Occupy Nation: The Roots, the Spirit, and the Promise of Occupy Wall Street* (2012).

Rose K. Goldsen (1917–85) was a professor of sociology at Cornell University and collaborator of Paul Lazarsfeld and a former colleague of Mills. With Mills and Clarence Ollson Senior, she coauthored *The Puerto Rican Journey* (1950). Lazarsfeld's critiques of *The Sociological Imagination* were printed in his foreword to Goldsen's book *What College Students Think* (1960).

Alvin Ward Gouldner (1920–80) was a prominent sociologist whose intellectual project has been compared to that of Mills. Formerly a functionalist and a Marxist, he later became a proponent of "reflexive sociology." His most celebrated work is *The Coming Crisis of Western Sociology* (1970).

William Franklin "Billy" Graham (b. 1918) is an American evangelist minister. He rose to fame during the 1950s, when his sermons were first broadcast on radio and television.

Tom Hayden (b. 1939) is a left-wing social activist most famous for his role in protests against the Vietnam War (1955–75). He has also written numerous books including *The Long Sixties: From 1960 to Barack Obama* (2009).

George C. Homans (1910–89), an American sociologist, is often considered the founder of social exchange theory. Works include *The Human Group*, *Social Behavior: Its Elementary Forms* (1950).

Irving Louis Horowitz (1929–2012), an American sociologist known for his work on genocide, was responsible for editing four volumes of C. Wright Mills's essays and also produced a biography: *C. Wright Mills: An American Utopian* (1983). Like Mills, he wrote a fierce critique of sociology, *The Decomposition of Sociology* (1993).

Paul Felix Lazarsfeld (1901–76) was an Austrian American sociologist who focused on the development of statistical techniques of social analysis. He had a powerful influence on modern American sociology, steering it toward applied empirical studies. His major works are collected into *An Empirical Theory of Social Action* (2011).

Rhonda Levine recently retired as a professor of sociology at Colgate University. Her best-known book, which she edited, is *Social Class and Stratification: Classic Statements and Theoretical Debates* (1998).

Seymour Lipset (1922–2006) was an American political sociologist. Perhaps his most enduring contribution was his theory that democracy is a result of economic prosperity. This argument was made in *Political Man: The Social Bases of Politics* (1960).

Herbert Marcuse (1898–1979) was a prominent German sociologist and philosopher of the critical Frankfurt school. His most famous works include *The One Dimensional Man* (1964) and *A Study on Authority* (1936).

Karl Marx (1818–83) was a German philosopher, political economist, and historian who is widely regarded as one of the founders of modern social sciences. His best-known works include *The German Ideology* (1846), *The Manifesto of the Communist Party* (1848), and *Capital* (1867). He has arguably been the most influential critic of capitalism, and his theories have informed most socialist movements worldwide.

Joseph McCarthy (1908–57) was a US senator between 1947 and 1957. He was notorious for his claim, in 1950, to have a list of socialist spies and saboteurs who were holding important positions in the US government. He never gave proof of this claim.

Robert K. Merton (1910–2003) was a prominent American sociologist, known for proposing "middle range" theories as a replacement for the big theoretical systems of classical sociology. His most famous works include *Social Theory and Social Structure* (1964), and *The Self-Fulfilling Prophecy* (1948).

Ralph Miliband (1924–94) was one of Britain's best-known sociologists. He was a key member of the New Left and authored works including *Socialism for a Sceptical Age* (1994).

Barrington Moore, Jr. (1913–2005) was an American political sociologist famous for his work on modernization. His most famous work is *Social Origins of Dictatorship and Democracy: Lord and Peasant in the Making of the Modern World* (1966).

Martin Oppenheimer (b. 1930) is professor emeritus of sociology at Rutgers University, and is also a civil rights and peace activist. *The Urban Guerrilla* (1969) and *White Collar Politics* (1985) are among his better-known works.

Talcott Parsons (1902–79) was among the best-known theorists of American sociology in his time. He was the author of classic texts such as *The Structure of Social Action* (1937), *The Social System* (1951), and *Social Structure and Personality* (1964).

Edward A. Ross (1866–1951) was an American sociologist and a supporter of eugenics. His works included *Social Control: A Survey of the Foundations of Order* (1901).

Edward Shils (1910–95) was an American sociologist and professor at the University of Chicago. An influential functionalist, he coauthored with Talcott Parsons *Toward a General Theory of Action* (1951).

Neil Smelser (b. 1930) is an American sociologist well known for (among other things) his work on collective behavior. Talcott Parsons supervised his PhD thesis at Harvard. His works include *Social Change in the Industrial Revolution: An Application of Theory to The British Cotton Industry* (1959).

Alexis de Tocqueville (1805–59) was a French historian and political theorist. He is most famous for his timeless *Democracy in America* (1835), generally recognized as one of the first examples of sociological analysis.

Thorstein Bunde Veblen (1857–1929) was an American economist and sociologist; he was an acid critic of capitalism, but rejected Marxism. His most famous work is *The Theory of the Leisure Class* (1899).

Max Weber (1864–1920) was a German sociologist and political economist. He is considered one of the foundational thinkers of sociology, and particularly of the "interpretative paradigm" in the social sciences. His most famous titles are *The Protestant Ethic and the Spirit of Capitalism* (1905) and *Economy and Society* (1922), the latter a posthumous collection of notes and essays.

WORKS CITED

WORKS CITED

Aronowitz, Stanley. *Taking It Big: C. Wright Mills and the Making of Political Intellectuals*. New York: Columbia University Press, 2012.

Beck, Ulrich. *Risk Society: Towards a New Modernity.* London: Sage Publications, 1992.

Beck, Ulrich, Wolfgang Bonss, and Christoph Lau. "The Theory of Reflexive Modernization: Problematic, Hypotheses and Research Programme." *Theory, Culture & Society* 20, no. 2 (2003): 1–33. Accessed January 12, 2016. doi:10.1177/0263276403020002001.

Bell, Daniel. *The End of Ideology: On the Exhaustion of Political Ideas in the Fifties.* Cambridge, MA: Harvard University Press, 1988.

Bierstedt, Robert. "Review of *The New Sociology*." *American Sociological Review* 30, no. 2 (1965): 274–5.

Bourdieu, Pierre. *In Other Words: Essays Towards a Reflexive Sociology.* Stanford, CA: Stanford University Press, 1990.

Bressler, Marvin. "*The Sociological Imagination* by C. Wright Mills." *Annals of the American Academy of Political and Social Science* 326 (1959): 181–2.

Brewer, John D. "Imagining *The Sociological Imagination*: The Biographical Context of a Sociological Classic." *British Journal of Sociology* 55, no. 3 (2004): 317–33.

Burawoy, Michael. "2004 American Sociological Association Presidential address: For Public Sociology." *The British Journal of Sociology* 56, no. 2 (2005): 259–94. Accessed January 12, 2016. doi:10.1111/j.1468-4446.2005.00059.x.

"Critical Sociology: A Dialogue between Two Sciences." *Contemporary Sociology* 27, no. 1 (1998): 12–20.

"Open Letter to C. Wright Mills." *Antipode* 40, no. 3 (2008): 365–75. Accessed January 12, 2016. doi:10.1111/j.1467-8330.2008.00602.x.

"The Return of the Repressed: Recovering the Public Face of U.S. Sociology, One Hundred Years On." *Annals of the American Academy of Political and Social Science* 600 (2005): 68–85.

Calhoun, Craig J., ed. *Sociology in America: A History*. Chicago: University of Chicago Press, 2007.

Dandaneau, Steven P. "Sisyphus Had It Easy: Reflections of Two Decades of Teaching the Sociological Imagination." *Teaching Sociology* 37, no. 1 (2009): 8–19.

Davis, Arthur K. "Review of *The New Sociology*." *Annals of the American Academy of Political and Social Science* 359 (1965): 205–6.

Denzin, Norman K. "Presidential Address on *The Sociological Imagination* Revisited." *The Sociological Quarterly* 31, no. 1 (1990): 1–22.

Derber, Charles. "The Mind of the Moralist: Review of *C. Wright Mills: An American Utopian*." *Contemporary Sociology* 13, no. 3 (1984): 273–5.

Eldridge, John. *C. Wright Mills.* New York: Tavistock Publications, 1983.

Flacks, Dick. "The Sociology Liberation Movement: Some Legacies and Lessons." *Critical Sociology* 15, no. 2 (1988): 9–18. Accessed January 12, 2016. doi:10.1177/089692058801500202.

Fletcher, Ronald. "*The Sociological Imagination* by C. Wright Mills." *The British Journal of Sociology* 11, no. 2 (1960): 169–70.

Floud, Jean. "*The Sociological Imagination* by C. Wright Mills." *British Journal of Educational Studies* 9, no. 1 (1960): 75–6.

Form, William. "Memories of C. Wright Mills: Social Structure and Biography." *Work and Occupations* 34, no. 2 (2007).

Foucault, Michel. *Discipline and Punish: The Birth of the Prison*. New York: Vintage, 1975.

The History of Sexuality. New York: Vintage, 1976.

Frost, Mervyn. "The Role of Normative Theory in IR." *Millennium – Journal of International Studies* 23, no. 1 (1994): 109–18. Accessed January 12, 2016. doi:10.1177/03058298940230010701.

Geary, Daniel. "Becoming International Again: C. Wright Mills and the Emergence of a Global New Left, 1956–1962." *The Journal of American History* 95, no. 3 (2008): 710–36.

Radical Ambition: C. Wright Mills, the Left, and American Social Thought. Berkeley: University of California Press, 2009.

Gill, Timothy M. "'Why Mills, Not Gouldner?' Selective History and Differential Commemoration in Sociology." *The American Sociologist* 44, no. 1 (2013): 96–115.

Gillam, Richard. "'White Collar' from Start to Finish: C. Wright Mills in Transition." *Theory and Society* 10, no. 1 (1981): 1–30.

Gitlin, Todd. Afterword to *The Sociological Imagination*, by C. Wright Mills, 229–42. New York: Oxford University Press, 2000.

Goldsen, Rose K. *What College Students Think*. Princeton, NJ: Van Nostrand, 1960.

Goldthorpe, John H. *On Sociology*. 2nd ed. 2 vols. Stanford, CA: Stanford University Press, 2007.

Google Scholar. "C. Wright Mills." Accessed January 13, 2016. https://scholar.google.co.uk/citations?user=dqBi45AAAAAJ&hl=en&oi=ao

Gouldner, Alvin W. *The Coming Crisis of Western Sociology*. New York: Basic Books, 1970.

Homans, George. "*The Sociological Imagination* by C. Wright Mills." *American Journal of Sociology* 65, no. 5 (1960): 517–8.

Horowitz, Irving L. *C. Wright Mills: An American Utopian*. New York: The Free Press, 1983.

"In Memoriam: *The Sociological Imagination* of C. Wright Mills." *American Journal of Sociology* 68, no. 1 (1962): 105–7.

ed. *The New Sociology: Essays in Social Science and Social Theory in Honor of C. Wright Mills*. New York: Oxford University Press, 1964.

House, Floyd N. "Review of *The New Sociology*." *Social Forces* 43, no. 2 (1964): 264–5.

Illing, Hans A. "*The Sociological Imagination* by C. Wright Mills." *The Journal of Criminal Law, Criminology, and Police Science* 51, no. 1 (1960): 87–8.

International Sociological Association. "Books of the Century." Accessed January 13, 2016. http://www.isa-sociology.org/books/vt/bkv_000.htm

Jamison, Andrew and Eyerman, Ron. *Seeds of the Sixties*. Berkeley: University of California Press, 1995.

Kerr, Keith. *Postmodern Cowboy: C. Wright Mills and a New 21st-Century Sociology*. Boulder, CO: Paradigm Publishers, 2008.

Lazarsfeld, Paul F. Foreword to *What College Students Think* by Rose K. Goldsen. Princeton, NJ: Van Nostrand, 1960.

Marsh, Ian, ed. *Theory and Practice in Sociology*. Harlow: Pearson Education, 2002.

Marx, Karl. *Economic and Philosophic Manuscripts of 1844*. Buffalo, NY: Prometheus Books, 1988.

Mills, C. Wright. "The Professional Ideology of Social Pathologists." *American Journal of Sociology* 49, no. 2 (1943): 165–80.

"The Powerless People: The Social Role of the Intellectual." *Bulletin of the American Association of University Professors* 31, no. 2 (1944): 231–43.

"The Intellectual and the Labor Leader." In *The Politics of Truth: Selected Writings of C. Wright Mills*, edited by John H. Summers, 25–32. New York: Oxford University Press, 2008.

The New Men of Power: America's Labor Leaders. Urbana, IL: University of Illinois Press, 1948.

White Collar: The American Middle Classes. 5th edition. New York: Oxford University Press, 2002.

"The Theory of the Leisure Class." In *The Politics of Truth: Selected Writings of C. Wright Mills*, edited by John H. Summers, 63–78. New York: Oxford University Press, 2008.

"Two Styles of Research in Current Social Studies." *Philosophy of Science* 20, no. 4 (1953): 266–75.

"IBM Plus Researching Plus Humanism = Sociology." In *The Politics of Truth: Selected Writings of C. Wright Mills*, edited by John H. Summers, 79–86. New York: Oxford University Press, 2008.

The Power Elite. New York: Oxford University Press, 1956.

"Growing Up: Facts and Fancies." In *Letters and Autobiographical Writings*, edited by Kathryn Mills and Pamela Mills, 24–30. Berkeley: University of California Press, 2000.

The Causes of World War Three. New York: M. E. Sharpe, 1985.

The Sociological Imagination. New York: Oxford University Press, 2000.

Listen, Yankee The Revolution in Cuba. New York: McGraw-Hill, 1960.

The Marxists. Harmondsworth: Penguin Books, 1962.

Letters and Autobiographical Writings. Edited by Kathryn Mills and Pamela Mills. Berkeley: University of California Press, 2000.

Pitch, Tamar. "The Roots of Radical Sociology." *Critical Sociology* 4, no. 4 (1974): 45–58.

Rosenberg, Justin. "The International Imagination: IR Theory and 'Classic Social Analysis.'" *Millennium – Journal of International Studies* 23, no. 1 (1994): 85–108.

Roucek, Joseph S. "Review of *The New Sociology*." *The Western Political Quarterly* 17, no. 3 (1964): 554–5.

Rytina, Steven. "Youthful Vision, Youthful Promise, Through Midlife Bifocals: C. Wright Mills' 'White Collar' Turns 50." *Sociological Forum* 16, no. 3 (2001): 563–74.

Shils, Edward. "Professor Mills on the Calling of Sociology." *World Politics* 13, no. 4 (1961): 600–21.

Smith, Steve. "Rearranging the Deckchairs on the Ship Called Modernity: Rosenberg, Epistemology and Emancipation." *Millennium – Journal of International Studies* 23, no. 2 (1994): 395–405.

Summers, John H. "The Epigone's Embrace: Irving Louis Horowitz on C. Wright Mills." *Minnesota Review* 68 (2007): 107–124. Accessed January 13, 2016. doi:10.1215/00265667-2007-68-107.

"The Epigone's Embrace, Part II: C. Wright Mills and The New Left." *Left History* 13, no. 2 (2008): 94–127.

"New Man of Power." In *The Politics of Truth: Selected Writings of C. Wright Mills*, 3–12. New York: Oxford University Press, 2008.

ed. *The Politics of Truth: Selected Writings of C. Wright Mills*. New York: Oxford University Press, 2008.

Treviño, A.J. *The Social Thought of C. Wright Mills*. Thousand Oaks, CA: Pine Forge Press, 2012.

Weber, Max. *The Protestant Ethic and the Spirit of Capitalism*. 3rd ed. Los Angeles: Roxbury Publishing Co., 2002.

Economy and Society: An Outline of Interpretive Sociology. 2 vols. Reprint, Berkeley and Los Angeles: University of California Press, 1978.

THE MACAT LIBRARY
BY DISCIPLINE

AFRICANA STUDIES

Chinua Achebe's *An Image of Africa: Racism in Conrad's Heart of Darkness*
W. E. B. Du Bois's *The Souls of Black Folk*
Zora Neale Huston's *Characteristics of Negro Expression*
Martin Luther King Jr's *Why We Can't Wait*
Toni Morrison's *Playing in the Dark: Whiteness in the American Literary Imagination*

ANTHROPOLOGY

Arjun Appadurai's *Modernity at Large: Cultural Dimensions of Globalisation*
Philippe Ariès's *Centuries of Childhood*
Franz Boas's *Race, Language and Culture*
Kim Chan & Renée Mauborgne's *Blue Ocean Strategy*
Jared Diamond's *Guns, Germs & Steel: the Fate of Human Societies*
Jared Diamond's *Collapse: How Societies Choose to Fail or Survive*
E. E. Evans-Pritchard's *Witchcraft, Oracles and Magic Among the Azande*
James Ferguson's *The Anti-Politics Machine*
Clifford Geertz's *The Interpretation of Cultures*
David Graeber's *Debt: the First 5000 Years*
Karen Ho's *Liquidated: An Ethnography of Wall Street*
Geert Hofstede's *Culture's Consequences: Comparing Values, Behaviors, Institutes and Organizations across Nations*
Claude Lévi-Strauss's *Structural Anthropology*
Jay Macleod's *Ain't No Makin' It: Aspirations and Attainment in a Low-Income Neighborhood*
Saba Mahmood's *The Politics of Piety: The Islamic Revival and the Feminist Subjec*t
Marcel Mauss's *The Gift*

BUSINESS

Jean Lave & Etienne Wenger's *Situated Learning*
Theodore Levitt's *Marketing Myopia*
Burton G. Malkiel's *A Random Walk Down Wall Street*
Douglas McGregor's *The Human Side of Enterprise*
Michael Porter's *Competitive Strategy: Creating and Sustaining Superior Performance*
John Kotter's *Leading Change*
C. K. Prahalad & Gary Hamel's *The Core Competence of the Corporation*

CRIMINOLOGY

Michelle Alexander's *The New Jim Crow: Mass Incarceration in the Age of Colorblindness*
Michael R. Gottfredson & Travis Hirschi's *A General Theory of Crime*
Richard Herrnstein & Charles A. Murray's *The Bell Curve: Intelligence and Class Structure in American Life*
Elizabeth Loftus's *Eyewitness Testimony*
Jay Macleod's *Ain't No Makin' It: Aspirations and Attainment in a Low-Income Neighborhood*
Philip Zimbardo's *The Lucifer Effect*

ECONOMICS

Janet Abu-Lughod's *Before European Hegemony*
Ha-Joon Chang's *Kicking Away the Ladder*
David Brion Davis's *The Problem of Slavery in the Age of Revolution*
Milton Friedman's *The Role of Monetary Policy*
Milton Friedman's *Capitalism and Freedom*
David Graeber's *Debt: the First 5000 Years*
Friedrich Hayek's *The Road to Serfdom*
Karen Ho's *Liquidated: An Ethnography of Wall Street*

The Macat Library By Discipline

John Maynard Keynes's *The General Theory of Employment, Interest and Money*
Charles P. Kindleberger's *Manias, Panics and Crashes*
Robert Lucas's *Why Doesn't Capital Flow from Rich to Poor Countries?*
Burton G. Malkiel's *A Random Walk Down Wall Street*
Thomas Robert Malthus's *An Essay on the Principle of Population*
Karl Marx's *Capital*
Thomas Piketty's *Capital in the Twenty-First Century*
Amartya Sen's *Development as Freedom*
Adam Smith's *The Wealth of Nations*
Nassim Nicholas Taleb's *The Black Swan: The Impact of the Highly Improbable*
Amos Tversky's & Daniel Kahneman's *Judgment under Uncertainty: Heuristics and Biases*
Mahbub Ul Haq's *Reflections on Human Development*
Max Weber's *The Protestant Ethic and the Spirit of Capitalism*

FEMINISM AND GENDER STUDIES

Judith Butler's *Gender Trouble*
Simone De Beauvoir's *The Second Sex*
Michel Foucault's *History of Sexuality*
Betty Friedan's *The Feminine Mystique*
Saba Mahmood's *The Politics of Piety: The Islamic Revival and the Feminist Subject*
Joan Wallach Scott's *Gender and the Politics of History*
Mary Wollstonecraft's *A Vindication of the Rights of Woman*
Virginia Woolf's *A Room of One's Own*

GEOGRAPHY

The Brundtland Report's *Our Common Future*
Rachel Carson's *Silent Spring*
Charles Darwin's *On the Origin of Species*
James Ferguson's *The Anti-Politics Machine*
Jane Jacobs's *The Death and Life of Great American Cities*
James Lovelock's *Gaia: A New Look at Life on Earth*
Amartya Sen's *Development as Freedom*
Mathis Wackernagel & William Rees's *Our Ecological Footprint*

HISTORY

Janet Abu-Lughod's *Before European Hegemony*
Benedict Anderson's *Imagined Communities*
Bernard Bailyn's *The Ideological Origins of the American Revolution*
Hanna Batatu's *The Old Social Classes And The Revolutionary Movements Of Iraq*
Christopher Browning's *Ordinary Men: Reserve Police Batallion 101 and the Final Solution in Poland*
Edmund Burke's *Reflections on the Revolution in France*
William Cronon's *Nature's Metropolis: Chicago And The Great West*
Alfred W. Crosby's *The Columbian Exchange*
Hamid Dabashi's *Iran: A People Interrupted*
David Brion Davis's *The Problem of Slavery in the Age of Revolution*
Nathalie Zemon Davis's *The Return of Martin Guerre*
Jared Diamond's *Guns, Germs & Steel: the Fate of Human Societies*
Frank Dikotter's *Mao's Great Famine*
John W Dower's *War Without Mercy: Race And Power In The Pacific War*
W. E. B. Du Bois's *The Souls of Black Folk*
Richard J. Evans's *In Defence of History*
Lucien Febvre's *The Problem of Unbelief in the 16th Century*
Sheila Fitzpatrick's *Everyday Stalinism*

Eric Foner's *Reconstruction: America's Unfinished Revolution, 1863-1877*
Michel Foucault's *Discipline and Punish*
Michel Foucault's *History of Sexuality*
Francis Fukuyama's *The End of History and the Last Man*
John Lewis Gaddis's *We Now Know: Rethinking Cold War History*
Ernest Gellner's *Nations and Nationalism*
Eugene Genovese's *Roll, Jordan, Roll: The World the Slaves Made*
Carlo Ginzburg's *The Night Battles*
Daniel Goldhagen's *Hitler's Willing Executioners*
Jack Goldstone's *Revolution and Rebellion in the Early Modern World*
Antonio Gramsci's *The Prison Notebooks*
Alexander Hamilton, John Jay & James Madison's *The Federalist Papers*
Christopher Hill's *The World Turned Upside Down*
Carole Hillenbrand's *The Crusades: Islamic Perspectives*
Thomas Hobbes's *Leviathan*
Eric Hobsbawm's *The Age Of Revolution*
John A. Hobson's *Imperialism: A Study*
Albert Hourani's *History of the Arab Peoples*
Samuel P. Huntington's *The Clash of Civilizations and the Remaking of World Order*
C. L. R. James's *The Black Jacobins*
Tony Judt's *Postwar: A History of Europe Since 1945*
Ernst Kantorowicz's *The King's Two Bodies: A Study in Medieval Political Theology*
Paul Kennedy's *The Rise and Fall of the Great Powers*
Ian Kershaw's *The "Hitler Myth": Image and Reality in the Third Reich*
John Maynard Keynes's *The General Theory of Employment, Interest and Money*
Charles P. Kindleberger's *Manias, Panics and Crashes*
Martin Luther King Jr's *Why We Can't Wait*
Henry Kissinger's *World Order: Reflections on the Character of Nations and the Course of History*
Thomas Kuhn's *The Structure of Scientific Revolutions*
Georges Lefebvre's *The Coming of the French Revolution*
John Locke's *Two Treatises of Government*
Niccolò Machiavelli's *The Prince*
Thomas Robert Malthus's *An Essay on the Principle of Population*
Mahmood Mamdani's *Citizen and Subject: Contemporary Africa And The Legacy Of Late Colonialism*
Karl Marx's *Capital*
Stanley Milgram's *Obedience to Authority*
John Stuart Mill's *On Liberty*
Thomas Paine's *Common Sense*
Thomas Paine's *Rights of Man*
Geoffrey Parker's *Global Crisis: War, Climate Change and Catastrophe in the Seventeenth Century*
Jonathan Riley-Smith's *The First Crusade and the Idea of Crusading*
Jean-Jacques Rousseau's *The Social Contract*
Joan Wallach Scott's *Gender and the Politics of History*
Theda Skocpol's *States and Social Revolutions*
Adam Smith's *The Wealth of Nations*
Timothy Snyder's *Bloodlands: Europe Between Hitler and Stalin*
Sun Tzu's *The Art of War*
Keith Thomas's *Religion and the Decline of Magic*
Thucydides's *The History of the Peloponnesian War*
Frederick Jackson Turner's *The Significance of the Frontier in American History*
Odd Arne Westad's *The Global Cold War: Third World Interventions And The Making Of Our Times*

LITERATURE

Chinua Achebe's *An Image of Africa: Racism in Conrad's Heart of Darkness*
Roland Barthes's *Mythologies*
Homi K. Bhabha's *The Location of Culture*
Judith Butler's *Gender Trouble*
Simone De Beauvoir's *The Second Sex*
Ferdinand De Saussure's *Course in General Linguistics*
T. S. Eliot's *The Sacred Wood: Essays on Poetry and Criticism*
Zora Neale Huston's *Characteristics of Negro Expression*
Toni Morrison's *Playing in the Dark: Whiteness in the American Literary Imagination*
Edward Said's *Orientalism*
Gayatri Chakravorty Spivak's *Can the Subaltern Speak?*
Mary Wollstonecraft's *A Vindication of the Rights of Women*
Virginia Woolf's *A Room of One's Own*

PHILOSOPHY

Elizabeth Anscombe's *Modern Moral Philosophy*
Hannah Arendt's *The Human Condition*
Aristotle's *Metaphysics*
Aristotle's *Nicomachean Ethics*
Edmund Gettier's *Is Justified True Belief Knowledge?*
Georg Wilhelm Friedrich Hegel's *Phenomenology of Spirit*
David Hume's *Dialogues Concerning Natural Religion*
David Hume's *The Enquiry for Human Understanding*
Immanuel Kant's *Religion within the Boundaries of Mere Reason*
Immanuel Kant's *Critique of Pure Reason*
Søren Kierkegaard's *The Sickness Unto Death*
Søren Kierkegaard's *Fear and Trembling*
C. S. Lewis's *The Abolition of Man*
Alasdair MacIntyre's *After Virtue*
Marcus Aurelius's *Meditations*
Friedrich Nietzsche's *On the Genealogy of Morality*
Friedrich Nietzsche's *Beyond Good and Evil*
Plato's *Republic*
Plato's *Symposium*
Jean-Jacques Rousseau's *The Social Contract*
Gilbert Ryle's *The Concept of Mind*
Baruch Spinoza's *Ethics*
Sun Tzu's *The Art of War*
Ludwig Wittgenstein's *Philosophical Investigations*

POLITICS

Benedict Anderson's *Imagined Communities*
Aristotle's *Politics*
Bernard Bailyn's *The Ideological Origins of the American Revolution*
Edmund Burke's *Reflections on the Revolution in France*
John C. Calhoun's *A Disquisition on Government*
Ha-Joon Chang's *Kicking Away the Ladder*
Hamid Dabashi's *Iran: A People Interrupted*
Hamid Dabashi's *Theology of Discontent: The Ideological Foundation of the Islamic Revolution in Iran*
Robert Dahl's *Democracy and its Critics*
Robert Dahl's *Who Governs?*
David Brion Davis's *The Problem of Slavery in the Age of Revolution*

Alexis De Tocqueville's *Democracy in America*
James Ferguson's *The Anti-Politics Machine*
Frank Dikotter's *Mao's Great Famine*
Sheila Fitzpatrick's *Everyday Stalinism*
Eric Foner's *Reconstruction: America's Unfinished Revolution, 1863-1877*
Milton Friedman's *Capitalism and Freedom*
Francis Fukuyama's *The End of History and the Last Man*
John Lewis Gaddis's *We Now Know: Rethinking Cold War History*
Ernest Gellner's *Nations and Nationalism*
David Graeber's *Debt: the First 5000 Years*
Antonio Gramsci's *The Prison Notebooks*
Alexander Hamilton, John Jay & James Madison's *The Federalist Papers*
Friedrich Hayek's *The Road to Serfdom*
Christopher Hill's *The World Turned Upside Down*
Thomas Hobbes's *Leviathan*
John A. Hobson's *Imperialism: A Study*
Samuel P. Huntington's *The Clash of Civilizations and the Remaking of World Order*
Tony Judt's *Postwar: A History of Europe Since 1945*
David C. Kang's *China Rising: Peace, Power and Order in East Asia*
Paul Kennedy's *The Rise and Fall of Great Powers*
Robert Keohane's *After Hegemony*
Martin Luther King Jr.'s *Why We Can't Wait*
Henry Kissinger's *World Order: Reflections on the Character of Nations and the Course of History*
John Locke's *Two Treatises of Government*
Niccolò Machiavelli's *The Prince*
Thomas Robert Malthus's *An Essay on the Principle of Population*
Mahmood Mamdani's *Citizen and Subject: Contemporary Africa And The Legacy Of Late Colonialism*
Karl Marx's *Capital*
John Stuart Mill's *On Liberty*
John Stuart Mill's *Utilitarianism*
Hans Morgenthau's *Politics Among Nations*
Thomas Paine's *Common Sense*
Thomas Paine's *Rights of Man*
Thomas Piketty's *Capital in the Twenty-First Century*
Robert D. Putman's *Bowling Alone*
John Rawls's *Theory of Justice*
Jean-Jacques Rousseau's *The Social Contract*
Theda Skocpol's *States and Social Revolutions*
Adam Smith's *The Wealth of Nations*
Sun Tzu's *The Art of War*
Henry David Thoreau's *Civil Disobedience*
Thucydides's *The History of the Peloponnesian War*
Kenneth Waltz's *Theory of International Politics*
Max Weber's *Politics as a Vocation*
Odd Arne Westad's *The Global Cold War: Third World Interventions And The Making Of Our Times*

POSTCOLONIAL STUDIES

Roland Barthes's *Mythologies*
Frantz Fanon's *Black Skin, White Masks*
Homi K. Bhabha's *The Location of Culture*
Gustavo Gutiérrez's *A Theology of Liberation*
Edward Said's *Orientalism*
Gayatri Chakravorty Spivak's *Can the Subaltern Speak?*

The Macat Library By Discipline

PSYCHOLOGY

Gordon Allport's *The Nature of Prejudice*
Alan Baddeley & Graham Hitch's *Aggression: A Social Learning Analysis*
Albert Bandura's *Aggression: A Social Learning Analysis*
Leon Festinger's *A Theory of Cognitive Dissonance*
Sigmund Freud's *The Interpretation of Dreams*
Betty Friedan's *The Feminine Mystique*
Michael R. Gottfredson & Travis Hirschi's *A General Theory of Crime*
Eric Hoffer's *The True Believer: Thoughts on the Nature of Mass Movements*
William James's *Principles of Psychology*
Elizabeth Loftus's *Eyewitness Testimony*
A. H. Maslow's *A Theory of Human Motivation*
Stanley Milgram's *Obedience to Authority*
Steven Pinker's *The Better Angels of Our Nature*
Oliver Sacks's *The Man Who Mistook His Wife For a Hat*
Richard Thaler & Cass Sunstein's *Nudge: Improving Decisions About Health, Wealth and Happiness*
Amos Tversky's *Judgment under Uncertainty: Heuristics and Biases*
Philip Zimbardo's *The Lucifer Effect*

SCIENCE

Rachel Carson's *Silent Spring*
William Cronon's *Nature's Metropolis: Chicago And The Great West*
Alfred W. Crosby's *The Columbian Exchange*
Charles Darwin's *On the Origin of Species*
Richard Dawkin's *The Selfish Gene*
Thomas Kuhn's *The Structure of Scientific Revolutions*
Geoffrey Parker's *Global Crisis: War, Climate Change and Catastrophe in the Seventeenth Century*
Mathis Wackernagel & William Rees's *Our Ecological Footprint*

SOCIOLOGY

Michelle Alexander's *The New Jim Crow: Mass Incarceration in the Age of Colorblindness*
Gordon Allport's *The Nature of Prejudice*
Albert Bandura's *Aggression: A Social Learning Analysis*
Hanna Batatu's *The Old Social Classes And The Revolutionary Movements Of Iraq*
Ha-Joon Chang's *Kicking Away the Ladder*
W. E. B. Du Bois's *The Souls of Black Folk*
Émile Durkheim's *On Suicide*
Frantz Fanon's *Black Skin, White Masks*
Frantz Fanon's *The Wretched of the Earth*
Eric Foner's *Reconstruction: America's Unfinished Revolution, 1863-1877*
Eugene Genovese's *Roll, Jordan, Roll: The World the Slaves Made*
Jack Goldstone's *Revolution and Rebellion in the Early Modern World*
Antonio Gramsci's *The Prison Notebooks*
Richard Herrnstein & Charles A Murray's *The Bell Curve: Intelligence and Class Structure in American Life*
Eric Hoffer's *The True Believer: Thoughts on the Nature of Mass Movements*
Jane Jacobs's *The Death and Life of Great American Cities*
Robert Lucas's *Why Doesn't Capital Flow from Rich to Poor Countries?*
Jay Macleod's *Ain't No Makin' It: Aspirations and Attainment in a Low Income Neighborhood*
Elaine May's *Homeward Bound: American Families in the Cold War Era*
Douglas McGregor's *The Human Side of Enterprise*
C. Wright Mills's *The Sociological Imagination*

Thomas Piketty's *Capital in the Twenty-First Century*
Robert D. Putman's *Bowling Alone*
David Riesman's *The Lonely Crowd: A Study of the Changing American Character*
Edward Said's *Orientalism*
Joan Wallach Scott's *Gender and the Politics of History*
Theda Skocpol's *States and Social Revolutions*
Max Weber's *The Protestant Ethic and the Spirit of Capitalism*

THEOLOGY

Augustine's *Confessions*
Benedict's *Rule of St Benedict*
Gustavo Gutiérrez's *A Theology of Liberation*
Carole Hillenbrand's *The Crusades: Islamic Perspectives*
David Hume's *Dialogues Concerning Natural Religion*
Immanuel Kant's *Religion within the Boundaries of Mere Reason*
Ernst Kantorowicz's *The King's Two Bodies: A Study in Medieval Political Theology*
Søren Kierkegaard's *The Sickness Unto Death*
C. S. Lewis's *The Abolition of Man*
Saba Mahmood's *The Politics of Piety: The Islamic Revival and the Feminist Subject*
Baruch Spinoza's *Ethics*
Keith Thomas's *Religion and the Decline of Magic*

COMING SOON

Chris Argyris's *The Individual and the Organisation*
Seyla Benhabib's *The Rights of Others*
Walter Benjamin's *The Work Of Art in the Age of Mechanical Reproduction*
John Berger's *Ways of Seeing*
Pierre Bourdieu's *Outline of a Theory of Practice*
Mary Douglas's *Purity and Danger*
Roland Dworkin's *Taking Rights Seriously*
James G. March's *Exploration and Exploitation in Organisational Learning*
Ikujiro Nonaka's *A Dynamic Theory of Organizational Knowledge Creation*
Griselda Pollock's *Vision and Difference*
Amartya Sen's *Inequality Re-Examined*
Susan Sontag's *On Photography*
Yasser Tabbaa's *The Transformation of Islamic Art*
Ludwig von Mises's *Theory of Money and Credit*

Macat Disciplines

Access the greatest ideas and thinkers across entire disciplines, including

MAN AND THE ENVIRONMENT

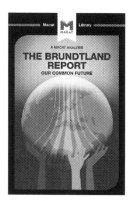

The Brundtland Report's, *Our Common Future*
Rachel Carson's, *Silent Spring*
James Lovelock's, *Gaia: A New Look at Life on Earth*
Mathis Wackernagel & William Rees's, *Our Ecological Footprint*

Macat analyses are available from all good bookshops and libraries.

Access hundreds of analyses through one, multimedia tool.
Join free for one month **library.macat.com**

Macat Disciplines

*Access the greatest ideas and thinkers
across entire disciplines, including*

MACAT

THE FUTURE OF DEMOCRACY

Robert A. Dahl's, *Democracy and Its Critics*
Robert A. Dahl's, *Who Governs?*
Alexis De Toqueville's, *Democracy in America*
Niccolò Machiavelli's, *The Prince*
John Stuart Mill's, *On Liberty*
Robert D. Putnam's, *Bowling Alone*
Jean-Jacques Rousseau's, *The Social Contract*
Henry David Thoreau's, *Civil Disobedience*

Macat analyses are available from all good bookshops and libraries.

Access hundreds of analyses through one, multimedia tool.
Join free for one month **library.macat.com**

Macat Disciplines

Access the greatest ideas and thinkers across entire disciplines, including

TOTALITARIANISM

Sheila Fitzpatrick's, *Everyday Stalinism*
Ian Kershaw's, *The "Hitler Myth"*
Timothy Snyder's, *Bloodlands*

Macat analyses are available from all good bookshops and libraries.

Access hundreds of analyses through one, multimedia tool.
Join free for one month **library.macat.com**

Macat Pairs

Analyse historical and modern issues from opposite sides of an argument. Pairs include:

RACE AND IDENTITY

Zora Neale Hurston's
Characteristics of Negro Expression

Using material collected on anthropological expeditions to the South, Zora Neale Hurston explains how expression in African American culture in the early twentieth century departs from the art of white America. At the time, African American art was often criticized for copying white culture. For Hurston, this criticism misunderstood how art works. European tradition views art as something fixed. But Hurston describes a creative process that is alive, ever-changing, and largely improvisational. She maintains that African American art works through a process called 'mimicry'—where an imitated object or verbal pattern, for example, is reshaped and altered until it becomes something new, novel—and worthy of attention.

Frantz Fanon's
Black Skin, White Masks

Black Skin, White Masks offers a radical analysis of the psychological effects of colonization on the colonized.

Fanon witnessed the effects of colonization first hand both in his birthplace, Martinique, and again later in life when he worked as a psychiatrist in another French colony, Algeria. His text is uncompromising in form and argument. He dissects the dehumanizing effects of colonialism, arguing that it destroys the native sense of identity, forcing people to adapt to an alien set of values—including a core belief that they are inferior. This results in deep psychological trauma.

Fanon's work played a pivotal role in the civil rights movements of the 1960s.

Macat analyses are available from all good bookshops and libraries.

Access hundreds of analyses through one, multimedia tool.
Join free for one month **library.macat.com**

Macat Pairs

Analyse historical and modern issues from opposite sides of an argument. Pairs include:

MACAT

MACAT

INTERNATIONAL RELATIONS IN THE 21ST CENTURY

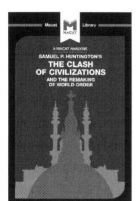

Samuel P. Huntington's
The Clash of Civilisations

In his highly influential 1996 book, Huntington offers a vision of a post-Cold War world in which conflict takes place not between competing ideologies but between cultures. The worst clash, he argues, will be between the Islamic world and the West: the West's arrogance and belief that its culture is a "gift" to the world will come into conflict with Islam's obstinacy and concern that its culture is under attack from a morally decadent "other."

Clash inspired much debate between different political schools of thought. But its greatest impact came in helping define American foreign policy in the wake of the 2001 terrorist attacks in New York and Washington.

Francis Fukuyama's
The End of History and the Last Man

Published in 1992, *The End of History and the Last Man* argues that capitalist democracy is the final destination for all societies. Fukuyama believed democracy triumphed during the Cold War because it lacks the "fundamental contradictions" inherent in communism and satisfies our yearning for freedom and equality. Democracy therefore marks the endpoint in the evolution of ideology, and so the "end of history." There will still be "events," but no fundamental change in ideology.

Macat analyses are available from all good bookshops and libraries.

Access hundreds of analyses through one, multimedia tool.
Join free for one month **library.macat.com**

Printed in the United States
by Baker & Taylor Publisher Services